G U I D E

Reporting on Controls at a Service Organization

Relevant to Security, Availability, Processing Integrity, Confidentiality, or Privacy (SOC 2)

MAY 1, 2011

1 2 3 4 5 6 7 8 9 0 AAP 1 9 8 7 6 5 4 3 2 1

ISBN 978-0-87051-960-4

Notice to Readers

This AICPA Guide was prepared by the Trust/Data Integrity Task Force and the Privacy Task Force of the Assurance Services Executive Committee of the AICPA to assist CPAs in performing examinations under AT section 101, *Attest Engagements* (AICPA, *Professional Standards*), to report on a service organization's controls over its system relevant to security, availability, processing integrity, confidentiality, or privacy. The Auditing Standards Board (ASB) has found the descriptions of attestation standards, procedures, and practices in this guide to be consistent with existing standards covered by Rule 202, *Compliance With Standards* (AICPA, *Professional Standards*, ET sec. 202 par. .01), and Rule 203, *Accounting Principles* (AICPA, *Professional Standards*, ET sec. 203 par. .01).

Attestation guidance included in an AICPA guide is an interpretive publication pursuant to AT section 50, *SSAE Hierarchy* (AICPA, *Professional Standards*). *Interpretive publications* are recommendations on the application of Statements on Standards for Attestation Engagements (SSAEs) in specific circumstances, including engagements performed for entities in specialized industries. An interpretive publication is issued under the authority of the ASB after all ASB members have been provided with an opportunity to consider and comment on whether the proposed interpretive publication is consistent with the SSAEs. The members of the ASB have found this guide to be consistent with existing SSAEs.

A practitioner[1] should be aware of and consider interpretive publications applicable to his or her examination. If a practitioner does not apply the attestation guidance included in an applicable interpretive publication, the practitioner should be prepared to explain how he or she complied with the SSAE provisions addressed by such attestation guidance.

Auditing Standards Board (2010–2011)

Darrel R. Schubert, *Chair*	Thomas A. Ratcliffe
Ernest F. Baugh, Jr.	Brian R. Richson
Brian R. Bluhm	Thomas M. Stemlar
Robert E. Chevalier	Mark H. Taylor
Samuel K. Cotterell	Kim L. Tredinnick
James R. Dalkin	H. Steven Vogel
David D. Duree	Phil D. Wedemeyer
Edwin G. Jolicoeur	Kurtis Wolff
David M. Morris	Megan F. Zietsman
Kenneth R. Odom	

---

[1] In the attestation standards, a CPA performing an attestation engagement ordinarily is referred to as a *practitioner*. Statement on Standards for Attestation Engagements No. 16, *Reporting on Controls at a Service Organization* (AICPA, *Professional Standards*, AT sec. 801), uses the term *service auditor*, rather than *practitioner*, to refer to a CPA reporting on controls at a service organization, as does this guide.

Preface

Purpose and Applicability

This guide has been prepared to assist CPAs engaged to examine and report on a service organization's controls over one or more of the following:

- The security of a service organization's system
- The availability of a service organization's system
- The processing integrity of a service organization's system
- The confidentiality of the information that the service organization's system processes or maintains for user entities
- The privacy of personal information that the service organization collects, uses, retains, discloses, and disposes of for user entities

The engagement described in this guide is based on the requirements and guidance established in AT section 101, *Attest Engagements* (AICPA, *Professional Standards*). Statements on Standards for Attestation Engagements (SSAEs) are also known as the attestation standards. The attestation standards enable a practitioner to report on subject matter other than financial statements. AT section 101 provides a framework for all attestation engagements.

A practitioner may be engaged to examine and report on controls at a service organization related to various types of subject matter (for example, controls that affect user entities' financial reporting or the privacy of information processed for user entities' customers). The applicable attestation standard for such engagements may vary, depending on the subject matter. To make practitioners aware of the various professional standards and guides available to them for examining and reporting on controls at a service organization and to help practitioners select the appropriate standard or guide for a particular engagement, the AICPA has introduced the term *service organization controls (SOC) reports*. The following are designations for three such engagements and the source of the guidance for performing and reporting on them:

- SOC 1: SSAE No. 16, *Reporting on Controls at a Service Organization* (AICPA, *Professional Standards*, AT sec. 801), and the AICPA Guide *Service Organizations: Applying SSAE No. 16,* Reporting on Controls at a Service Organization
- SOC 2: The AICPA Guide *Reporting on Controls at a Service Organization Relevant to Security, Availability, Processing Integrity, Confidentiality, or Privacy*
- SOC 3: TSP section 100, *Trust Services Principles, Criteria, and Illustrations for Security, Availability, Processing Integrity, Confidentiality, and Privacy* (AICPA, *Technical Practice Aids*)

This guide focuses on SOC 2 engagements. Paragraph 1.24 of this guide includes a table that compares features of the three engagements.

TABLE OF CONTENTS

Contents

Chapter 1

Introduction and Background

This chapter explains the relationship between a service organization and its user entities, provides examples of service organizations, identifies the criteria that are used to evaluate the design and operating effectiveness of controls at a service organization, explains the difference between a type 1 and type 2 service auditor's report, and presents three reporting options for CPAs reporting on controls at a service organization.

1.01 Many entities function more efficiently and profitably by outsourcing tasks or entire functions to other organizations that have the personnel, expertise, equipment, or technology to accomplish these tasks or functions. This guide focuses on organizations that collect, process, transmit, store, organize, maintain, or dispose of information for other entities. In this guide, organizations that operate information systems and provide services to other entities are known as *service organizations*, and entities that use the services of service organizations are known as *user entities*. Examples of the services provided by such service organizations are as follows:

- *Cloud computing.* Providing on-demand network access to a shared pool of configurable computing resources (for example, networks, servers, storage, applications, and services). (Additional information about cloud computing is presented in appendix E, "Reporting on Controls at a Cloud Computing Service Organization.")

- *Managed security.* Managing access to networks and computing systems for user entities (for example, granting access to a system and preventing, or detecting and mitigating, system intrusion).

- *Financial services customer accounting.* Processing financial transactions on behalf of customers of a bank or investment company. Examples of this service are processing customer securities transactions, maintaining customer account records, providing customers with confirmations of transactions and statements, and providing these and related customer services through the Internet.

- *Customer support.* Providing customers of user entities with online or telephonic postsales support and service management. Examples of these services are warranty inquiries and investigating and responding to customer complaints.

- *Sales force automation.* Providing and maintaining software to automate business tasks for user entities that have a sales force. Examples of such tasks are order processing, information sharing, order tracking, contact management, customer management, sales forecast analysis, and employee performance evaluation.

- *Health care claims management and processing.* Providing medical providers, employers, and insured parties of employers with systems that enable medical records and related health insurance claims to be processed securely and confidentially.

- *Enterprise IT outsourcing services.* Managing, operating, and maintaining user entities' IT data centers, infrastructure, and application systems and related functions that support IT activities, such as network, production, security, change management, hardware, and environmental control activities.

1.02 Management of a user entity is responsible for assessing and addressing risks faced by the user entity related to financial reporting, compliance with laws and regulations, and the efficiency and effectiveness of operations. When a user entity engages a service organization to perform key processes or functions, the user entity exposes itself to additional risks related to the service organization's system. Although management of a user entity can delegate tasks or functions to a service organization, the responsibility for the product or service provided to customers of the user entity cannot be delegated. Management of the user entity is usually held responsible by those charged with governance (for example, the board of directors); customers; shareholders; regulators; and other affected parties for establishing effective internal control over outsourced functions.

1.03 To assess and address the risks associated with an outsourced service, management of the user entity needs information about the service organization's controls[1] over the system through which the services are provided. When assessing controls at a service organization that may be relevant to and affect the services provided to user entities, management of a user entity may ask the service organization for a CPA's report on the design and operating effectiveness of controls over the service organization's system that may be relevant to the security, availability, or processing integrity of the system (security, availability, processing integrity) or the confidentiality or privacy of the information processed for user entities (confidentiality or privacy).

1.04 Footnote 1 of TSP section 100, *Trust Services Principles, Criteria, and Illustrations for Security, Availability, Processing Integrity, Confidentiality, and Privacy* (AICPA, *Technical Practice Aids*), contains the following definition of a system:

A *system* consists of five key components organized to achieve a specified objective. The five components are categorized as follows:

- *Infrastructure.* The physical and hardware components of a system (facilities, equipment, and networks)
- *Software.* The programs and operating software of a system (systems, applications, and utilities)
- *People.* The personnel involved in the operation and use of a system (developers, operators, users, and managers)
- *Procedures.* The automated and manual procedures involved in the operation of a system
- *Data.* The information used and supported by a system (transaction streams, files, databases, and tables)

1.05 Statements on Standards for Attestation Engagements (SSAEs)—also known as the attestation standards—enable a CPA to report on subject

---

[1] In this guide, *controls* are policies and procedures that enable an entity to meet specified criteria.

matter other than financial statements. Most of the attestation standards address specific subject matter, such as reporting on an entity's compliance with laws and regulations or on a financial forecast or projection. AT section 101, *Attest Engagements* (AICPA, *Professional Standards*), however, provides a framework for performing and reporting on all attestation engagements.

1.06 TSP section 100 provides criteria for evaluating and reporting on controls related to security, availability, processing integrity, confidentiality, and privacy. In TSP section 100, these five attributes of a system are known as *principles*, and they are defined in paragraph .10 of TSP section 100 as follows:

 a. Security. The system is protected against unauthorized access (both physical and logical).

 b. Availability. The system is available for operation and use as committed or agreed.

 c. Processing integrity. System processing is complete, accurate, timely, and authorized.

 d. Confidentiality. Information designated as confidential is protected as committed or agreed.

 e. Privacy. Personal information[2] is collected, used, retained, disclosed, and destroyed[3] in conformity with the commitments in the entity's privacy notice[4] and with criteria set forth in generally accepted privacy principles (GAPP) issued by the AICPA and CICA.[5] [The criteria in GAPP are the same as the criteria for the privacy principle in TSP section 100.]

1.07 The primary focus of this guide is on examining and reporting on a description of a service organization's system and the suitability of the design and operating effectiveness of its controls relevant to security availability, processing integrity, confidentiality, or privacy. Paragraphs 1.08–.09 describe two related engagements and are included here to provide context and background for the engagement that is the primary focus of this guide.

---

[2] [Personal information is information that is about or can be related to an identifiable individual.]

[3] [Collection, use, retention, disclosure, and disposal or anonymization are the aspects of the personal information life cycle.]

[4] [Entities that collect personal information generally establish and document their policies regarding the nature of the information they collect and how that information will be used, retained, disclosed, and disposed of or anonymized. These policies and the entity's commitment to adhere to them when included in a written communication to individuals about whom personal information is collected (sometimes referred to as *data subjects*) are referred to as a *privacy notice*. A privacy notice also includes information about such matters as the purpose of collecting the information; the choices individuals have related to their personal information; the security of such information; and how individuals can contact the entity with inquiries, complaints, and disputes related to their personal information. When a user entity collects personal information from individuals, it typically provides a privacy notice to those individuals.

When a service organization is involved in any of the phases of the personal information life cycle, it may or may not be responsible for providing a privacy notice to the individuals about whom information is collected. If the user entity is responsible for providing the privacy notice, the service organization provides a statement of privacy practices to the user entities that includes the same types of policies and commitments as would be included in a privacy notice, but the statement is written from the perspective of the service organization communicating its privacy-related policies and commitments to the user entities. The statement of privacy practices provides a basis for the user entities to prepare a privacy notice to be sent to individuals or for ensuring that the service organization has appropriate practices for meeting the existing privacy commitments of user entities.]

[5] [The criteria for the content of a statement of privacy practices are set forth in paragraphs 1.33–.34 of this guide.]

Service Organization Control 3 Reports Under TSP Section 100 - By anyone. No DETAILED DESCRIPTION OF AUDITOR'S TESTS + Result

1.08 The guidance in TSP section 100 for performing and reporting on an examination engagement using the trust services criteria is based on AT section 101. A practitioner may report on one or more of the five trust services principles (principles). In the examination report included in TSP section 100, the practitioner expresses an opinion on whether the service organization maintained effective controls over its system, based on the criteria in TSP section 100 that are applicable to the principle(s) being reported on. In this guide, the examination engagement described in TSP section 100 is known as a *service organization controls (SOC) 3 engagement*, and the resulting report is known as a *SOC 3 report*. Although a SOC 3 report is designed to meet the needs of a broad range of users, it does not contain a detailed description of the service auditor's tests of the operating effectiveness of controls and the results of those tests, which may be necessary for a particular user to determine how it is affected by those controls.

SOC 1 Reports Under SSAE No. 16

1.09 SSAE No. 16, *Reporting on Controls at a Service Organization* (AICPA, *Professional Standards*, AT sec. 801),[6] establishes the requirements and guidance for a CPA examining and reporting on a service organization's description of its system and its controls that are likely to be relevant to user entities' internal control over financial reporting. Service organizations frequently receive requests from user entities for these reports because they are needed by the auditors of the user entities' financial statements (user auditors) to obtain information about controls at the service organization that may affect assertions in the user entities' financial statements. In this guide, an engagement performed under SSAE No. 16 is known as a *SOC 1 engagement*, and a report on that engagement is known as a *SOC 1 report*. SOC 1 reports are intended solely for the information and use of existing user entities (for example, existing customers of the service organization); their financial statement auditors; and management of the service organization.

SOC 2 Reports Under AT Section 101 and the AICPA Guide *Reporting on Controls at a Service Organization Relevant to Security, Availability, Processing Integrity, Confidentiality, or Privacy*

1.10 Although SSAE No. 16 is intended only for reporting on controls at a service organization that are likely to be relevant to user entities' internal

---

[6] Statement on Auditing Standards (SAS) No. 70, *Service Organizations* (AICPA, *Professional Standards*, AU sec. 324), addresses the user auditor's responsibility for obtaining sufficient appropriate audit evidence in an audit of the financial statements of a user entity. Prior to the issuance of Statement on Standards for Attestation Engagements (SSAE) No. 16, *Reporting on Controls at a Service Organization* (AICPA, *Professional Standards*, AT sec. 801), the applicable requirements and guidance for both service auditors and user auditors was included in SAS No. 70. The requirements and guidance for service auditors was moved to SSAE No. 16. The requirements and guidance for user auditors is retained in AU section 324, *Service Organizations* (AICPA, *Professional Standards*). When the clarified SAS *Audit Considerations Relating to an Entity Using a Service Organization* becomes effective, it will replace the guidance for user auditors currently in AU section 324. The clarified SAS is effective for audits of financial statements for periods ending on or after December 15, 2012.

control over financial reporting, paragraph .02 of SSAE No. 16 indicates that the guidance in SSAE No. 16 may be helpful to a practitioner[7] performing an engagement under AT section 101 to report on a service organization's controls other than those that are likely to be relevant to user entities' internal control over financial reporting. This guide establishes guidance for such an engagement—specifically, an examination engagement to report on controls at a service organization intended to mitigate risks related to security, availability, processing integrity, confidentiality, or privacy (trust services principles). In this guide, such an engagement is known as a *SOC 2 engagement,* and a report on that engagement is known as a *SOC 2 report.*

Trust Services Criteria

1.11 A service auditor may be engaged to report on a description of a service organization's system and the suitability of the design and operating effectiveness of controls relevant to one or more of the trust services principles listed in paragraph 1.06. The decision about which principles the description will address is usually made by management of the service organization and is often based on input from users.

1.12 In this guide, the criteria in TSP section 100 that are applicable to the principle(s) being reported on are known as the *applicable trust services criteria.* In a SOC 2 report, the service auditor expresses an opinion on the following:

- Whether the description of the service organization's system is fairly presented
- Whether the controls are suitably designed to provide reasonable assurance that the applicable trust services criteria would be met if the controls operated effectively
- In type 2 reports (described in paragraph 1.16[a]), whether the controls were operating effectively to meet the applicable trust services criteria
- In engagements to report on the privacy principle, whether the service organization complied with the commitments in its statement of privacy practices

1.13 The service auditor should determine that all of the applicable trust services criteria have been included in management's description. For example, if a service auditor is reporting on the design and operating effectiveness of controls at a service organization relevant to the security of user entities' information, the service auditor should determine that all of the criteria in the set of trust services criteria related to security have been included in the description. The applicable trust services criteria for each principle are presented in appendix B, "Trust Services Principles and Criteria for Security, Availability, Processing Integrity, Confidentiality, and Privacy," of this guide.

1.14 If one or more applicable trust services criteria have been omitted from the description, the service auditor should determine whether the description includes an explanation of why the criteria have been omitted, to meet the criteria in paragraph 1.33(a)(ix), and whether the applicable trust services criteria presented in the description should be considered complete. Omission of

---

[7] In the attestation standards, a CPA performing an attestation engagement ordinarily is referred to as a *practitioner.* SSAE No. 16 uses the term *service auditor,* rather than *practitioner,* to refer to a CPA reporting on controls at a service organization, as does this guide.

an applicable trust services criterion is appropriate if the omitted criterion is not applicable to the system that is the subject of the engagement. For example, consider an engagement that addresses the privacy principle in which personal information is collected from individuals by the user entities, not the service organization. In those circumstances, it would be appropriate for the service organization to omit the criteria related to the collection of personal information and describe the reason for such omission. However, the fact that a service organization has a policy or procedure to address certain applicable trust services criteria does not serve as justification for omitting those criteria. For example, in a report that addresses the privacy principle, it would not be appropriate for a service organization to omit criteria related to the disclosure of personal information to third parties because the service organization's policies forbid such disclosure.

1.15 Unlike SSAE No. 16, the primary users of SOC 2 reports generally are not user auditors but, rather, management of the service organization and management of the user entities. SOC 2 reports are intended to assist management of the user entities in carrying out their responsibility for monitoring the services provided by a service organization. For example, controls at a service organization that provides Internet-based storage of a user entity's backup of proprietary information and trade secrets is unlikely to be of significance to the user entity's financial statement auditor. However, management of the user entity may be particularly concerned about the security and confidentiality of the backed-up information. SOC 2 reports also may be useful to a user entity's internal auditors or practitioners reporting on a user entity's security, availability, processing integrity, confidentiality, or privacy. For example, a practitioner may be reporting on the privacy of the personal information of customers of a user entity and on the user entity's compliance with the commitments in its privacy notice. The practitioner may use a SOC 2 report that addresses the privacy principle that has been provided by the user entity's service organization as part of the evidence needed to report on the privacy of the user entity's customers' personal information.

Two Types of SOC 2 Reports

1.16 This guide provides for the following two types[8] of SOC 2 reports:

   a. Report on management's description of a service organization's system and the suitability of the design and operating effectiveness of controls (referred to in this guide as a *type 2 report*). This is a report that includes the following:

      i. Management's description of the service organization's system

      ii. A written assertion by management of the service organization[9] about whether, in all material respects

---

[8] SSAE No. 16 provides for the same two types of reports, but the subject matter is controls that may be relevant to user entities' internal control over financial reporting.

[9] Paragraph .09 of AT section 101, *Attest Engagements* (AICPA, *Professional Standards*), indicates that a practitioner should ordinarily obtain a written assertion in an examination or a review engagement. Paragraph .58 of AT section 101 states, in part

   If a written assertion cannot be obtained from the responsible party, the practitioner should consider the effects on his or her ability to obtain sufficient evidence to form a conclusion about the subject matter. When the practitioner's client is the responsible party, a failure to obtain

(continued)

(1) management's description of the service organization's system fairly presents the service organization's system that was designed and implemented throughout the specified period, based on the criteria in management's assertion (which are the criteria in paragraphs 1.33–.34).[10]

(2) the controls stated in management's description of the service organization's system were suitably designed throughout the specified period to meet the applicable trust services criteria

(3) the controls stated in management's description of the service organization's system operated effectively throughout the specified period to meet the applicable trust services criteria

(4) when the service organization's description of the system addresses the privacy principle, management of the service organization complied with the commitments in its statement of privacy practices throughout the specified period

iii. A service auditor's report that

(1) expresses an opinion on the matters in (a)(ii)(1)–(4) when the report covers the privacy principle

(2) includes a description of the service auditor's tests of controls and the results thereof, and when the report addresses the privacy principle, a description of the service auditor's tests of the service organization's compliance with the commitments in its statement of privacy practices and the results thereof

---

(footnote continued)

a written assertion should result in the practitioner concluding that a scope limitation exists [footnote omitted].

In evaluating the effect of the service auditor's inability to obtain a written assertion from management of the service organizaion, the service auditor should consider the following guidance in AT section 101:

.73 Restrictions on the scope of an engagement, whether imposed by the client or by such other circumstances as the timing of the work or the inability to obtain sufficient evidence, may require the practitioner to qualify the assurance provided, to disclaim any assurance, or to withdraw from the engagement. For example, if the practitioner's client is the responsible party, a failure to obtain a written assertion should result in the practitioner concluding that a scope limitation exists. (See paragraph .58.)

.74 The practitioner's decision to provide a qualified opinion, to disclaim an opinion, or to withdraw because of a scope limitation in an examination engagement depends on an assessment of the effect of the omitted procedure(s) on his or her ability to express assurance. This assessment will be affected by the nature and magnitude of the potential effects of the matters in question, and by their significance to the subject matter or the assertion. If the potential effects are pervasive to the subject matter or the assertion, a disclaimer or withdrawal is more likely to be appropriate. When restrictions that significantly limit the scope of the engagement are imposed by the client or the responsible party, the practitioner generally should disclaim an opinion or withdraw from the engagement. The reasons for a qualification or disclaimer should be described in the practitioner's report.

[10] These criteria are also included in appendix A, "Information for Management of a Service Organization," of this guide.

b. Report on management's description of a service organization's system and the suitability of the design of controls (referred to as a *type 1 report*). This is a report that includes the following:

    i. Management's description of the service organization's system

    ii. A written assertion by management of the service organization[11] about whether, in all material respects and based on suitable criteria

        (1) management's description of the service organization's system fairly presents the service organization's system that was designed and implemented as of a specified date, based on the criteria in paragraphs 1.33–.34

        (2) the controls stated in the description were suitably designed to meet the applicable trust services criteria as of a specified date

    iii. A service auditor's report that expresses an opinion on the matters in (b)(ii)(1)–(2)

In both a type 1 and type 2 engagement, to clearly communicate that management is responsible for the description of the service organization's system; the suitability of the design of the controls; and in a type 2 report, the operating effectiveness of the controls, management's written assertion is attached to the description of the service organization's system. When the report addresses the privacy principle, the statement of privacy practices should be included in, or attached to, the description.[12]

Difference Between SOC 2 and SOC 3 Reports

1.17 Although SOC 2 and SOC 3 reports address similar subject matter and use the same criteria (the criteria in TSP section 100), a SOC 2 report differs from a SOC 3 report in that a SOC 2 report provides report users with the following report components that are not included in a SOC 3 report:

- A description of the service organization's system prepared by management of the service organization[13]

- In a type 2 report, a description of the service auditor's tests of the operating effectiveness of the service organization's controls and the results of those tests

---

[11] See footnote 9.

[12] The criteria for a service organization's statement of privacy practices are presented in appendix A of this guide. In a type 1 and type 2 report, the service auditor's opinion on the fairness of the presentation of the description of the service organization's system also addresses the fairness of the presentation of the service organization's statement of privacy practices.

In a type 2 report, the service auditor expresses an opinion on the service organization's compliance with the commitments in its statement of privacy practices. In a type 1 report, the service auditor does not express such an opinion.

[13] In a service organization controls (SOC) 3 report, management provides a description of the service organization's system and its boundaries. Typically, this description is less detailed than the description in a SOC 2 report. Also, the practitioner does not express an opinion on the fairness of the presentation of the description.

- In a type 2 report that addresses the privacy principle, a description of the service auditor's tests of the service organization's compliance with the commitments in its statement of privacy practices and the results of those tests

1.18 Another significant difference between a SOC 2 and SOC 3 report is that use of a SOC 2 report usually is intended for specified parties who are knowledgeable about the following:

- The nature of the service provided by the service organization
- How the service organization's system interacts with user entities, subservice organizations,[14] and other parties
- Internal control and its limitations
- The applicable trust services criteria, the risks that may prevent those criteria from being met, and how controls address those risks
- Complementary user-entity controls and how they interact with related controls at the service organization to meet the applicable trust services criteria

A SOC 3 report, however, ordinarily is a general-use report, which means that management of the service organization may provide the report to anyone. For that reason, management of a service organization may wish to engage a service auditor to perform and report on a SOC 2 and SOC 3 engagement to meet the governance needs of existing customers and market the service organization's services to prospective customers, which is a permitted use of a SOC 3 report. (See paragraph 1.19 for conditions that may preclude the service auditor from issuing an unqualified opinion in a SOC 3 engagement.)

1.19 The work performed in a SOC 2 engagement may enable a service auditor to report on a SOC 3 engagement, as well. However, because a SOC 3 engagement requires that all the applicable trust services criteria be met in order for the practitioner to issue an unqualified opinion, certain conditions would preclude the service auditor from issuing an unqualified SOC 3 opinion. The following are examples of such situations:

- An engagement in which the service organization has carved out subservice organizations from its system description. Under TSP section 100, the scope of the engagement would need to include all subservice organizations for which controls would need to be operating effectively to meet the applicable trust services criteria.
- An engagement in which complementary user-entity controls are significant to achieving the applicable trust services criteria. (See paragraph 1.20 for a discussion of complementary user-entity controls.) An example would be a service organization that provides managed security services to user entities that require the user entities to implement authentication procedures. Because the criteria cannot be entirely met by procedures implemented at the service organization, an unqualified opinion could not be issued.

---

[14] In this guide, a *subservice organization* is defined as a service organization used by another service organization to perform services related to the trust services principles. If a service organization uses a subservice organization, the description of the service organization's system may either (*a*) include the subservice organization's services, using the inclusive method, or (*b*) exclude the subservice organization's services, using the carve-out method.

1.20 In many cases, the applicable trust services criteria stated in the description cannot be met by implementing controls at a service organization alone and may require that user entities implement certain controls (complementary user-entity controls). If the implementation of complementary user-entity controls is necessary to meet specified applicable trust services criteria, the description should separately identify those complementary user-entity controls, along with the criteria that cannot be met by the service organization's controls alone. An example of a complementary user-entity control is a system designed with the assumption that user entities will have an authorized employee approve the accuracy of data prior to its submission to the service organization for processing.

1.21 A SOC 2 engagement is not intended to supersede or replace a SOC 3 engagement. In many instances, the detail in a description of a service organization's system and in the service auditor's description of tests of controls is not needed by report users. In that case, a SOC 3 engagement may be a better option.

Trust Services Criteria for SOC 2 and SOC 3 Engagements and Control Objectives for SOC 1 Engagements

1.22 In SOC 2 and SOC 3 engagements, the criteria used to evaluate whether controls were suitably designed or operating effectively are the applicable trust services criteria. Accordingly, in every SOC 2 and SOC 3 engagement that addresses the same principle(s), the criteria will be the same (the applicable trust services criteria). However, in a SOC 1 engagement, the service auditor evaluates whether the service organization's controls were suitably designed or operating effectively by determining whether the control objectives specified by management of the service organization were achieved.[15] SSAE No. 16 requires that the control objectives for a SOC 1 report be reasonable in the circumstances. Although most service organizations providing like services will have similar control objectives, in order for control objectives to be reasonable in the circumstances, they should reflect features of the particular service organization, such as the nature of the services provided and the industries in which the user entities operate. Accordingly, in SOC 1 engagements, not all service organizations will have the same control objectives.

Combining SOC 1 and SOC 2 Reports Not Permitted

1.23 A service organization's controls may be relevant to a user entity's internal control over financial reporting and also to the trust services principles. This guide is not intended to permit a SOC 2 report to be issued that combines reporting on a service organization's controls relevant to user entities' internal control over financial reporting with reporting on controls relevant to the trust services principles. A service organization may engage a service auditor to separately perform an engagement that addresses a service organization's controls related to user entities' internal control over financial reporting. If a service auditor is engaged to perform both a SOC 1 and SOC 2 engagement, certain testing performed in either engagement may provide evidence for the other engagement.

---

[15] SSAE No. 16 defines *control objectives* as the aim or purpose of specified controls at the service organization.

Comparison of SOC 1, SOC 2, and SOC 3 Engagements and Related Reports

1.24 The following table identifies differences between SOC 1, SOC 2, and SOC 3 reports:

	SOC 1 Reports	SOC 2 Reports	SOC 3 Reports
Under what professional standard is the engagement performed?	Statement on Standards for Attestation Engagements No. 16, *Reporting on Controls at a Service Organization* (AICPA, *Professional Standards*, AT sec. 801). The AICPA Guide *Service Organizations: Applying SSAE No. 16*, Reporting on Controls at a Service Organization.	AT section 101, *Attest Engagements* (AICPA, *Professional Standards*). The AICPA Guide *Reporting on Controls at a Service Organization Relevant to Security, Availability, Processing Integrity, Confidentiality, or Privacy*.	AT section 101. TSP section 100, *Trust Services Principles, Criteria, and Illustrations for Security, Availability, Processing Integrity, Confidentiality, and Privacy* (AICPA, *Technical Practice Aids*), provides the criteria for evaluating the design and operating effectiveness of controls in these engagements, as well as the criteria for the content of a privacy notice.
What is the subject matter of the engagement?	Controls at a service organization relevant to user entities' internal control over financial reporting.	Controls at a service organization relevant to security, availability, processing integrity, confidentiality, or privacy. If the report addresses the privacy principle, the service organization's compliance with the commitments in its statement of privacy practices.	Controls at a service organization relevant to security, availability, processing integrity, confidentiality, or privacy. If the report addresses the privacy principle, the service organization's compliance with the commitments in its privacy notice.[16]
What is the purpose of the report?	To provide the auditor of a user entity's financial statements with information and a CPA's opinion about controls at a service organization that may be relevant to a user entity's internal	To provide management of a service organization, user entities, and other specified parties with information and a CPA's opinion about controls at the service organization relevant to security,	To provide interested parties with a CPA's opinion about controls at the service organization relevant to security, availability, processing integrity, confidentiality, or privacy.

(continued)

---

[16] See the second paragraph of footnote 4 in this chapter for an explanation of the difference between a privacy notice and a statement of privacy practices.

	SOC 1 Reports	*SOC 2 Reports*	*SOC 3 Reports*
	control over financial reporting. It enables the user auditor to perform risk assessment procedures and, if a type 2 report is provided, to use the report as audit evidence that controls at the service organization are operating effectively.	availability, processing integrity, confidentiality, or privacy. A type 2 report that addresses the privacy principle also provides information and a CPA's opinion about the service organization's compliance with the commitments in its statement of privacy practices.	A report that addresses the privacy principle also provides a CPA's opinion about the service organization's compliance with the commitments in its privacy notice.
What are the components of the report?	A description of the service organization's system. A written assertion by management of the service organization regarding the description of the service organization's system; the suitability of the design of the controls; and in a type 2 report, the operating effectiveness of the controls in achieving the specified control objectives. A service auditor's report that contains an opinion on the fairness of the presentation of the description of the service organization's system; the suitability of the design of the controls to achieve specified control objectives; and in a type 2 report, the operating effectiveness of those controls.	A description of the service organization's system. A written assertion by management of the service organization regarding the description of the service organization's system; the suitability of the design of the controls; and in a type 2 report, the operating effectiveness of the controls in meeting the applicable trust services criteria. If the report addresses the privacy principle, the assertion also covers the service organization's compliance with the commitments in its statement of privacy practices. A service auditor's report that contains an opinion on the fairness of the presentation of the description of the service organization's system; the	A description of the system and its boundaries[17] or, in the case of a report that addresses the privacy principle, a copy of the service organization's privacy notice. A written assertion by management of the service organization regarding the effectiveness of controls in meeting the applicable trust services criteria and, if the report addresses the privacy principle, compliance with the commitments in the service organization's privacy notice. A service auditor's report on whether the entity maintained effective controls over its system as it relates to the principle being reported on (that is, security, availability, processing integrity,

---

[17] These descriptions are typically less detailed than the descriptions in SOC 1 or SOC 2 reports and are not covered by the practitioner's opinion.

	SOC 1 Reports	SOC 2 Reports	SOC 3 Reports
	In a type 2 report, a description of the service auditor's tests of the controls and the results of the tests.	suitability of the design of the controls to meet the applicable trust services criteria; and in a type 2 report, the operating effectiveness of those controls. If the report addresses the privacy principle, the service auditor's opinion on whether the service organization complied with the commitments in its statement of privacy practices. In a type 2 report, a description of the service auditor's tests of controls and the results of the tests. In a type 2 report that addresses the privacy principle, a description of the service auditor's tests of the service organization's compliance with the commitments in its statement of privacy practices and the results of those tests.	confidentiality, or privacy), based on the applicable trust services criteria. If the report addresses the privacy principle, the service auditor's opinion on whether the service organization complied with the commitments in its privacy notice.
Who are the intended users of the report?	Management of the service organization; user entities during some or all of the period covered by the report (for type 2 reports) and user entities as of a specified date (for type 1 reports); and auditors of the user entities' financial statements.	Management of the service organization and other specified parties who have sufficient knowledge and understanding of the following: • The nature of the service provided by the service organization • How the service organization's system interacts with user entities, subservice organizations, and other parties • Internal control and its limitations	Anyone

(continued)

	SOC 1 Reports	SOC 2 Reports	SOC 3 Reports
		• Complementary user-entity controls and how they interact with related controls at the service organization to meet the applicable trust services criteria • The applicable trust services criteria • The risks that may threaten the achievement of the applicable trust services criteria and how controls address those risks	

Boundaries of the System

1.25 In addition to the differences identified in the table in paragraph 1.24, SOC 1 engagements differ from SOC 2 engagements in other areas. For example, the boundaries of the systems addressed in SOC 2 engagements may be less apparent than the systems addressed in SOC 1 engagements, which address financial reporting systems or parts thereof. For that reason, the boundaries of a system addressed by a SOC 2 engagement need to be clearly understood, defined, and communicated. For example, a financial reporting system is likely to be bounded by the components of the system related to financial transaction initiation, authorization, recording, processing, and reporting. Whereas the boundaries of a system related to processing integrity (system processing is complete, accurate, timely, and authorized) may extend to other operations (for example, processes at customer call centers).

1.26 In a SOC 2 engagement that addresses the privacy principle, the system boundaries cover, at a minimum, all the system components, as they relate to the personal information life cycle, which consists of the collection, use, retention, disclosure, and disposal or anonymization of personal information, within well-defined processes and informal ad hoc procedures, such as e-mailing personal information to an actuary for retirement benefit calculations. The system boundaries would also include instances in which the personal information is combined with other information (for example, in a database or system), a process that would not otherwise cause the other information to be included in the scope of the engagement. That notwithstanding, the scope of a privacy engagement may be restricted to a business unit (online book sales) or geographical location (Canadian operations), as long as the personal information is not commingled with information from, or shared with, other business units or geographical locations.

Risks Addressed by Controls

1.27 Because of differences in the subject matter of SOC 1 and SOC 2 reports and the needs of intended report users, the risks and the controls that address those risks are likely to differ in SOC 1 and SOC 2 engagements.

For example, in a SOC 1 engagement, controls over changes to application programs would typically focus on risks related to unauthorized changes to the programs that could affect the financial reporting process. In a SOC 2 engagement that addresses the processing integrity principle, controls over program changes might need to cover the risks of unauthorized changes to a much broader range of application programs (for example, customer service applications and manufacturing process control applications).

Meaning of the Term *Security*

1.28 The term *security* may be interpreted more narrowly in a SOC 1 engagement than it would be in a SOC 2 engagement. For example, security in a SOC 1 engagement generally relates to the authorization of transactions and protection of the integrity of those transactions throughout the financial reporting process. In a SOC 1 engagement, protection of such information from unauthorized read access or disclosure may not be a concern. However, in a SOC 2 engagement that addresses the privacy or confidentiality principle, the term *security* relates to the authorization of transactions and protection of the integrity of those transactions throughout the system and also protecting personal and other information from unauthorized use or disclosure from the time it is collected until the time it is disposed of. In a SOC 2 engagement that addresses the availability principle, the term *security* may also relate to the protection of the system from interruptions in processing availability.

Difference Between Privacy and Security

1.29 Some individuals consider effective privacy practices to be the same as effective information security. However, privacy encompasses a much broader set of activities beyond security that contribute to the effectiveness of a privacy program, including, for example, providing users with the following:

- Notice of the service organization's privacy commitments and practices
- Choice regarding the use and disclosure of their personal information
- Access to their personal information for review and update
- An inquiry, complaint, and dispute resolution process[18]

Type 1 or Type 2 SOC 2 Reports

1.30 Because management of a user entity is responsible for assessing risks to the user entity and establishing and maintaining controls that address those risks, management of the user entity will need information about the design and operating effectiveness of controls at the service organization that affect the service provided to the user entity. A type 1 report does not include tests of the operating effectiveness of controls and the results thereof; therefore, it is unlikely to provide users with sufficient information to assess the effectiveness of controls at the service organization that address risks related to the outsourced service. However, a type 1 report may be useful to a user entity

---

[18] A definition of *privacy* and a further description of these activities are included in generally accepted privacy principles.

in understanding the service organization's system and controls. The following are circumstances in which a type 1 report may be useful:

- The service organization has not been in operation for a sufficient length of time to enable the service auditor to gather sufficient appropriate evidence regarding the operating effectiveness of controls.

- The service organization has recently made significant changes to the system and related controls and does not have a sufficient history with a stable system to enable a type 2 engagement to be performed.

Because of the limitations of a type 1 engagement, a service auditor may recommend that in such situations, a type 2 engagement covering a short period (for example, two months) be performed, rather than a type 1 engagement.

1.31 A service auditor's report may not include both a type 1 opinion for certain applicable trust services criteria and controls and a type 2 opinion for other applicable trust services criteria and controls. The service auditor is engaged to perform either a type 1 or type 2 engagement.

Contents of a SOC 2 Report

1.32 A type 2 SOC 2 report contains the service auditor's opinion about whether

- management's description of the service organization's system is fairly presented (see paragraphs 1.33–.34).

- the controls included in the description are suitably designed to meet the applicable trust services criteria stated in management's description (see paragraph 1.35).

- the controls included in the description were operating effectively to meet the applicable trust services criteria (see paragraph 1.36).

- for SOC 2 reports that address the privacy principle, management complied with the commitments in its statement of privacy practices throughout the specified period (see paragraph 1.37). (Management's statement of privacy practices should be included in, or attached to, management's description of the service organization's system.)

Criteria for Evaluating the Fairness of the Presentation of the Description

1.33 The criteria for determining whether the description of the service organization's system is fairly presented are as follows:

- *a.* The description contains the following information:
  - i. The types of services provided
  - ii. The components of the system used to provide the services, which are the following:
    - (1) *Infrastructure.* The physical and hardware components of a system (facilities, equipment, and networks).

— (2) *Software*. The programs and operating software of a system (systems, applications, and utilities).

— (3) *People*. The personnel involved in the operation and use of a system (developers, operators, users, and managers).

— (4) *Procedures*. The automated and manual procedures involved in the operation of a system.

— (5) *Data*. The information used and supported by a system (transaction streams, files, databases, and tables).

iii. The boundaries or aspects of the system covered by the description

iv. How the service organization's system captures and addresses significant events and conditions[19]

v. The process used to prepare and deliver reports and other information to user entities and other parties

vi. For information provided to, or received from, subservice organizations and other parties

(1) how the information is provided or received and the role of the subservice organizations and other parties

(2) the procedures the service organization performs to determine that such information and its processing, maintenance, and storage are subject to appropriate controls

vii. For each principle being reported on, the related criteria in TSP section 100 (applicable trust services criteria) and the related controls designed to meet those criteria, including, as applicable, the following:

(1) Complementary user-entity controls contemplated in the design of the service organization's system

(2) When the inclusive method is used to present a subservice organization, controls at the subservice organization

viii. If the service organization presents the subservice organization using the carve-out method

(1) the nature of the services provided by the subservice organization

(2) each of the applicable trust services criteria that are intended to be met by controls at the subservice organization, alone or in combination with controls at the service organization, and the types of controls expected to be implemented at carved-out subservice organizations to meet those criteria

---

[19] For example, the setup of access rights for new users of the system.

      ix. Any applicable trust services criteria that are not addressed by a control and the reasons therefore

      x. Other aspects of the service organization's control environment, risk assessment process, information and communication systems, and monitoring of controls that are relevant to the services provided and the applicable trust services criteria

      xi. In the case of a type 2 report, relevant details of changes to the service organization's system during the period covered by the description

   b. The description does not omit or distort information relevant to the service organization's system while acknowledging that the description is prepared to meet the common needs of a broad range of users and may not, therefore, include every aspect of the system that each individual user may consider important to its own particular needs.

1.34 If the description addresses controls over privacy, in addition to the criteria in paragraph 1.33 for determining whether the description of the service organization's system is fairly presented, the description should also include the following information:

   a. The types of personal information collected from individuals or obtained from user entities or other parties[20] and how such information is collected and, if collected by user entities, how it is obtained by the service organization

   b. The process for (i) identifying specific requirements in agreements with user entities and in laws and regulations applicable to the personal information and (ii) implementing controls and practices to meet those requirements

   c. If the service organization presents the subservice organization using the carve-out method

      i. any aspects of the personal information life cycle for which responsibility has been delegated to the subservice organization

      ii. the types of activities the subservice organization would need to perform to comply with the service organization's privacy commitments

   d. If the service organization provides the privacy notice to individuals about whom personal information is collected, used, retained, disclosed, and disposed of or anonymized, the privacy notice prepared in conformity with the relevant criteria for a privacy notice set forth in TSP section 100

   e. If the user entities, rather than the service organization, are responsible for providing the privacy notice to individuals, a statement regarding how the privacy notice is communicated to individuals, that the user entities are responsible for communicating such notice to individuals, and that the service organization is responsible for communicating its privacy practices to the user entities in its

---

[20] An example of an entity that collects personal information from user entities is a credit reporting bureau that maintains information about the creditworthiness of individuals.

statement of privacy practices, which includes the following information:

    i. A summary of the significant privacy and related security requirements common to most agreements between the service organization and its user entities and any requirements in a particular user entity's agreement that the service organization meets for all or most user entities

    ii. A summary of the significant privacy and related security requirements mandated by law, regulation, an industry, or a market that are not included in user entity agreements but the service organization meets for all or most user entities

    iii. The purposes, uses, and disclosures of personal information as permitted by user entity agreements and beyond those permitted by such agreements but not prohibited by such agreements and the service organization's commitments regarding the purpose, use, and disclosure of personal information that are prohibited by such agreements

    iv. A statement that the information will be retained for a period no longer than necessary to fulfill the stated purposes or contractual requirements or for the period required by law or regulation, as applicable, or a statement describing other retention practices

    v. A statement that the information will be disposed of in a manner that prevents loss, theft, misuse, or unauthorized access to the information

    vi. If applicable, how the service organization supports any process permitted by user entities for individuals to obtain access to their information to review, update, or correct it

    vii. If applicable, a description of the process to determine that personal information is accurate and complete and how the service organization implements correction processes permitted by user entities

    viii. If applicable, how inquiries, complaints, and disputes from individuals (whether directly from the individual or indirectly through user entities) regarding their personal information are handled by the service organization

    ix. A statement regarding the existence of a written security program and what industry or other standards it is based on

    x. Other relevant information related to privacy practices deemed appropriate for user entities by the service organization

  f. If the user entities, rather than the service organization, are responsible for providing the privacy notice to individuals, the service organization's statement of privacy practices.

1.35 The criterion for determining whether controls are suitably designed is that the controls identified in the description would, if operating as described, provide reasonable assurance that the applicable trust services criteria would be met.

1.36 The criterion for determining whether the controls identified in the description of the service organization's system operated effectively to meet the applicable trust services criterion is that the controls were consistently operated as designed throughout the specified period, including whether manual controls were applied by individuals who have the appropriate competence and authority.

1.37 In an engagement that addresses the privacy principle, the criterion for determining whether a service organization complied with the commitments in its statement of privacy practices is that the service organization collected, used, retained, disclosed, and disposed of or anonymized personal information in conformity with the commitments in its statement of privacy practices.

1.38 A service organization may request that the service auditor's report address additional subject matter that is not specifically covered by the criteria in this guide. An example of such subject matter is the service organization's compliance with certain criteria based on regulatory requirements (for example, security requirements under the Health Insurance Portability and Accountability Act of 1996) or compliance with performance criteria established in a service-level agreement. In order for a service auditor to report on such additional subject matter, the service organization provides the following:

- An appropriate supplemental description of the subject matter
- A description of the criteria used to measure and present the subject matter
- If the criteria are related to controls, a description of the controls intended to meet the control-related criteria
- An assertion by management regarding the additional subject matter

1.39 The service auditor should perform appropriate procedures related to the additional subject matter, in accordance with AT section 101 and the relevant guidance in this guide. The service auditor's description of the scope of the work and related opinion on the subject matter should be presented in separate paragraphs of the service auditor's report. In addition, based on the agreement with the service organization, the service auditor may include additional tests performed and detailed results of those tests in a separate attachment to the report.

Applying Certain Auditing Standards

1.40 The following AU sections relate to audits of financial statements; however, when relevant, they may be adapted and applied in performing a SOC 2 engagement:

- AU section 314, *Understanding the Entity and Its Environment and Assessing the Risks of Material Misstatement* (AICPA, *Professional Standards*)
- AU section 316, *Consideration of Fraud in a Financial Statement Audit* (AICPA, *Professional Standards*)
- AU section 322, *The Auditor's Consideration of the Internal Audit Function in an Audit of Financial Statements* (AICPA, *Professional Standards*)

- AU section 350, *Audit Sampling* (AICPA, *Professional Standards*)
- AU section 561, *Subsequent Discovery of Facts Existing at the Date of the Auditor's Report* (AICPA, *Professional Standards*)

Definitions

1.41 Definitions of the terms used in this guide are included in appendix D, "Definitions," of this guide. These definitions are similar to the definitions in SSAE No. 16; however, certain differences exist due to the difference in the subject matter addressed by SOC 1 and SOC 2 engagements.

Chapter 2

Planning a Service Auditor's Engagement

In planning a service auditor's engagement, management of the service organization and the service auditor each have specific responsibilities. This chapter describes the matters to be considered and procedures to be performed by the service auditor in planning the engagement. Appendix A, "Information for Management of a Service Organization," of this guide identifies management's responsibilities in a service auditor's engagement.

Responsibilities of Management of a Service Organization

2.01 When undergoing an examination of a description of a service organization's system and the design and operating effectiveness of controls, as described in this guide, management of a service organization is responsible for the following:

- Preparing a description of the service organization's system.

- Providing a written assertion.

- Determining the type of engagement to be performed; which principle(s) are addressed in the engagement; the scope of the engagement; and whether any subservice organizations will be included in, or carved out of, the description and service auditor's report.

- Providing written representations at the conclusion of the engagement. When the inclusive method is used, management of the service organization and management of the subservice organization agree to provide and do provide such representations.

- Having a reasonable basis for its assertion

Responsibilities of the Service Auditor

2.02 During planning, the service auditor is responsible for the following:

- Determining whether to accept or continue an engagement

- Reading the description of the service organization's system and obtaining an understanding of the system

- Establishing an understanding with management of the service organization, which ordinarily is documented in an engagement letter, regarding the services to be performed and the responsibilities of management and the service auditor

Engagement Acceptance and Continuance

2.03 A service auditor should accept or continue an engagement to report on controls at a service organization only if

a. the service auditor has the capabilities and competence to perform the engagement. Having relevant capabilities and competence to perform the engagement includes having

  i. adequate technical training and proficiency to perform an attestation engagement;

  ii. adequate knowledge of the subject matter;

  iii. reason to believe that the subject matter is capable of evaluation against criteria that are appropriate for the intended use;

  iv. knowledge of the service organization's industry and business;

  v. appropriate knowledge of systems and technology;

  vi. experience evaluating risks related to the suitability of the design of controls; and

  vii. experience evaluating the design of manual and IT controls related to the selected trust services principles, performing tests of such controls, and evaluating the results of the tests.

b. the service auditor is independent in mental attitude in all matters relating to the engagement and exercises due professional care in planning and performing the engagement and preparing the report.

c. the service auditor's preliminary knowledge of the engagement circumstances indicates that

  i. the criteria to be used will be suitable and available to the intended users of the report,

  ii. the service auditor will have access to sufficient and appropriate evidence to the extent necessary to conduct the engagement, and

  iii. the scope of the engagement and management's description of the service organization's system will not be so limited that they are unlikely to be useful to the intended users of the report. If the inclusive method is used, these conditions also apply with respect to the subservice organization.

2.04 Before accepting an engagement, the service auditor should consider the following:

- The integrity and reputation of management of the service organization and significant shareholders or principal owners

- The likelihood that association with the client will expose the service auditor to undue risk of damage to his or her professional reputation or financial loss or expose report users to misinformation and financial loss

2.05 The service auditor may obtain information about the matters in paragraph 2.04 by communicating with a predecessor service auditor, if any, regarding the reasons for change in service auditors, any disagreements between the predecessor auditor and service organization, and similar matters. The guidance in AU section 315, *Communications Between Predecessor and*

Successor Auditors (AICPA, *Professional Standards*), may be adapted and applied for this purpose. If the predecessor service auditor has issued a service auditor's report, it is not necessary for the service auditor to review the predecessor service auditor's working papers because of the detailed nature of the report.

2.06 As stated in paragraph 2.03(b), the service auditor should accept or continue an engagement to report on controls at a service organization only if the service auditor is independent of the service organization. Independence is required by the AICPA Code of Professional Conduct for examination engagements. Examples of relevant matters to consider when assessing independence are the scope of other services provided to the service organization, fee arrangements for all services, firm and individual financial relationships, firm business relationships, and alumni and familial relationships with the client and client personnel.

2.07 Paragraph .03 of ET section 92, *Definitions* (AICPA, *Professional Standards*), provides the following definition of a *client*: "A client is any person or entity, other than the member's employer, that engages a member or a member's firm to perform professional services or a person or entity with respect to which professional services are performed." Based on this definition, when management's description uses the inclusive method to present a subservice organization, the subservice organization would be considered a client because the service auditor has performed professional services with respect to the subservice organization. Consequently, the service auditor should be independent of the subservice organization.

2.08 The service auditor need not be independent of the users of the service organization.

2.09 Additional matters that are relevant when determining whether to accept or continue an engagement include the scope of the system being reported on, the functions performed by the system, how subservice organizations are used, how information about subservice organizations will be presented, the relevance of the trust services principle being reported on to the system, and the period covered by the report. Consideration should be given to these matters to determine whether the resulting report will be useful and not misleading to users of the report. For example, assume that management of the service organization wishes to engage the service auditor to perform a type 2 examination for a period of less than two months. In those circumstances, the service auditor should consider whether a report covering that period will be useful to users of the report, particularly if many of the controls related to the applicable trust services criteria are performed on a monthly or quarterly basis.

2.10 Another matter that the service auditor should consider when determining whether to accept or continue a service organization controls (SOC) 2 engagement is the intended users of the report. If the intended report users are unlikely to understand the nature of the engagement or the tests and results (for example, acceptable deviation rates or substantive tests versus tests of controls), a greater potential exists for the report to be misunderstood.

2.11 The service auditor may also consider whether management has realistic expectations about the engagement, particularly if it is likely that the report may require a qualification or other modification.

2.12 A service auditor may question accepting an engagement in which a service organization functions primarily as an intermediary between the user entities and subservice organization and performs few or no functions related to the service provided to user entities. If a service organization's controls do not contribute to meeting the applicable trust services criteria, a report on that service organization's controls is not likely to be useful to report users.

2.13 A service auditor ordinarily should accept or continue an engagement to report on controls at a service organization only if management of the service organization acknowledges and accepts responsibility for the following:

    a. Preparing its description of the service organization's system and its assertion, including the completeness, accuracy, and method of presentation of the description and assertion

    b. Providing a written assertion that will be attached to management's description of the service organization's system and provided to users

    c. Having a reasonable basis for its assertion

    d. Designing, implementing, and documenting controls that are suitably designed and operating effectively to provide reasonable assurance that the applicable trust services criteria are met

    e. Providing the service auditor with the following:

        i. Access to all information, such as records and documentation, including service level agreements, of which management is aware that is relevant to the description of the service organization's system and the assertion

        ii. Additional information that the service auditor may request from management for the purpose of the examination engagement

        iii. Unrestricted access to personnel within the service organization from whom the service auditor determines it is necessary to obtain evidence relevant to the service auditor's engagement

2.14 In preparing for an engagement in which the inclusive method will be used to present a subservice organization, the service auditor should obtain from the service organization written acknowledgement and acceptance by the subservice organization of its responsibility for the matters in paragraph 2.13.

2.15 When the inclusive method is used, the requirements and guidance in paragraphs 2.01–.14 also apply with respect to the subservice organization. Accordingly, during planning, the service auditor determines whether it will be possible to obtain an assertion from management of the subservice organization and evidence that supports the service auditor's opinion on the subservice organization's description of its system and the suitability of the design and operating effectiveness of the subservice organization's controls, including written representations from management of the subservice organization. If the subservice organization will not provide a written assertion and appropriate written representations, the service organization will be unable to use the inclusive method but may be able to use the carve-out method. Additional guidance on the inclusive method is provided in paragraphs 3.26–.28 of this guide.

Planning to Use the Work of the Internal Audit Function

2.16 The phrase *using the work of the internal audit function* is derived from AU section 322, *The Auditor's Consideration of the Internal Audit Function in an Audit of Financial Statements* (AICPA, *Professional Standards*), and it refers to work designed and performed by the internal audit function. This includes tests of controls designed and performed by the internal audit function during the period covered by the type 2 report and the results of those tests. This differs from work that the internal audit function performs to provide direct assistance to the service auditor, including assistance in performing tests of controls that are designed by the service auditor and performed by members of the internal audit function, under the direction, supervision, and review of the service auditor.

2.17 If the service organization has an internal audit function, the service auditor may obtain an understanding of the responsibilities and activities of the internal audit function to determine whether the work of the internal audit function is likely to be relevant to the engagement. The service auditor may obtain this understanding by making inquiries of appropriate management of the service organization and internal audit personnel. Examples of matters that may be important to this understanding are the internal audit function's

- organizational status within the service organization;
- application of, and adherence to, professional standards;
- audit plan, including the nature, timing, and extent of audit procedures; and
- access to records and whether limitations exist on the scope of the internal audit function's activities.

2.18 Work of the internal audit function that provides information or evidence about the fairness of the presentation of the description of the service organization's system, the suitability of the design of the controls, or the operating effectiveness of the controls that pertain to the trust services principle being reported on would be considered relevant to the engagement. The following are examples of information that may assist the service auditor in assessing the relevancy of that work:

- Knowledge gained from prior-year examinations related to the principle being reported on
- How management and the internal audit function assess risk related to the trust services principle being reported on and how audit resources are allocated to address those risks

2.19 Certain internal audit activities may not be relevant to a SOC 2 engagement (for example, the internal audit function's evaluation of the efficiency of certain management decision-making processes).

2.20 If, after obtaining an understanding of the internal audit function, the service auditor concludes that (*a*) the activities of the internal audit function are not relevant to the trust services principle being reported on, or (*b*) it may not be efficient to consider the work of the internal audit function, the service auditor does not need to give further consideration to the work of the internal audit function.

2.21 If the service auditor intends to use the work of the internal audit function or use internal audit personnel in a direct assistance capacity, the service auditor should determine whether the work performed by the internal audit function is likely to be adequate for the purposes of the engagement by evaluating the following:

 a. The objectivity and technical competence of the members of the internal audit function

 b. Whether the work of the internal audit function is likely to be carried out with due professional care

 c. Whether it is likely that effective communication will occur between the internal audit function and service auditor, including consideration of the effect of any constraints or restrictions placed on the internal audit function by the service organization.

2.22 If the service auditor determines that the work of the internal audit function is likely to be adequate for the purposes of the engagement, the service auditor should evaluate the following factors in determining the planned effect that the work of the internal audit function will have on the nature, timing, and extent of the service auditor's procedures:

 a. The nature and scope of specific work performed or to be performed by the internal audit function

 b. The significance of that work to the service auditor's conclusions

 c. The degree of subjectivity involved in the evaluation of the evidence gathered in support of those conclusions

Materiality

2.23 When planning and performing a SOC 2 engagement, the service auditor should evaluate materiality with respect to (a) the fair presentation of management's description of the service organization's system; (b) the suitability of the design of the controls; (c) in a type 2 engagement, the operating effectiveness of the controls; and (d) in a type 2 engagement that addresses the privacy principle, the service organization's compliance with the commitments in its statement of privacy practices. The concept of materiality takes into account that the report is intended to provide information to meet the common information needs of a broad range of users who understand the manner in which the system is being used. Materiality with respect to the service organization also applies to the subservice organization.

2.24 Materiality with respect to the fair presentation of management's description of the service organization's system and with respect to the design of controls primarily includes the consideration of qualitative factors. For example, whether

 • management's description of the service organization's system includes the significant aspects of system processing.

 • management's description of the service organization's system omits or distorts relevant information.

 • the controls have the ability, as designed, to provide reasonable assurance that the applicable trust services criteria stated in management's description of the service organization's system would be met.

2.25 Materiality with respect to the operating effectiveness of controls includes the consideration of both quantitative and qualitative factors (for example, the service auditor's tolerable rate and observed rate of deviation in the results of tests [a quantitative matter] and the nature and cause of any observed deviations [a qualitative matter]).

2.26 The concept of materiality is not applicable when disclosing in the description of tests of controls (and tests of compliance with privacy commitments, if applicable) the results of those tests for which deviations have been identified. This is because a deviation may have significance for a specific user entity beyond whether, in the opinion of the service auditor, it prevents a control from operating effectively. For example, the control to which the deviation relates may be particularly significant in preventing a certain type of error, the results of which may be material to a particular user entity but not other users.

Identifying Deviations

2.27 Before the service auditor begins tests of controls and tests of compliance, the service auditor should determine the procedures that will be performed and the circumstances under which a test result will be considered a deviation, so that all such results are reported as deviations in the description of tests of controls and tests of compliance.

Establishing an Understanding With the Client

2.28 Paragraph .46 of AT section 101, *Attest Engagements* (AICPA, *Professional Standards*), requires the practitioner to establish an understanding with the client regarding the services to be performed. That understanding should be documented in the working papers, preferably through a written communication with the client. Typically, this understanding is documented in an engagement letter. A documented understanding reduces the risk that either the service auditor or management of the service organization will misinterpret the needs or expectations of the other party. For example, it reduces the risk that management of the service organization will rely on the service auditor to protect the service organization from certain risks or perform certain management functions that are not part of the service auditor's responsibilities in a SOC 2 engagement.

2.29 The engagement letter typically includes the objectives of the engagement, a description of the services to be provided, the responsibilities of management of the service organization, the responsibilities of the service auditor, and the limitations of the engagement. Such matters as fees and timing may also be addressed in the engagement letter. If the service auditor believes that an understanding has not been established with management of the service organization, the service auditor would typically decline to accept or continue the engagement.

Chapter 3

Performing the Engagement

This chapter identifies matters that the service auditor considers and procedures that the service auditor performs to test (1) the fairness of the presentation of management's description of the service organization's system; (2) the suitability of the design of the controls included in the description; (3) in a type 2 report, the operating effectiveness of the controls included in the description; and (4) in a type 2 service organization controls (SOC) 2 engagement that addresses the privacy principle, whether the service organization complied with the commitments in its statement of privacy practices.

Obtaining and Evaluating Evidence About Whether the Description of the System is Fairly Presented

3.01 The service auditor should read the description of the service organization's system and perform procedures to determine whether the description is fairly presented. A description that is fairly presented should

- meet the criteria in paragraphs 1.33–.34 of this guide.
- describe the system as it was designed and implemented.
- include relevant details of changes to the system.

3.02 The procedures that the service auditor may perform to evaluate whether the description of the service organization's system is fairly presented typically include a combination of the following:

- Reading contracts and service level agreements with user entities to understand the nature and scope of the service provided by the service organization, as well as the service organization's contractual obligations to user entities
- Obtaining an understanding of the aspects of laws or regulations relevant to the services provided
- Observing the procedures performed by service organization personnel
- Reading service organization policy and procedure manuals and other documentation of the system (for example, flowcharts, narratives, and software and hardware asset management records)
- Performing walkthroughs of control activity-related policies and procedures and observing other system components
- Obtaining a list of user entities and determining how the services provided by the service organization are likely to affect the user entities (for example, determining the predominant type(s) of user entities, whether they are regulated entities, and the common types of services provided to the user entities)

- Discussing with management and other service organization personnel the content of management's assertion and the description of the service organization's system
- Reading reports of the internal audit function relevant to the principle being reported on

3.03 A conclusion that a description of a service organization's system is fairly presented does not imply that the controls included in the description are suitably designed or operating effectively to meet the applicable trust services criteria.

3.04 In determining whether the description of a service organization's system is fairly presented, the service auditor evaluates whether each control as presented provides sufficient information for users to understand how that control may affect the particular user. The description of a control generally will need to include the following information:

Relevant Information When Describing a Control	Example
The frequency with which the control is performed or the timing of its occurrence	Management reviews error reports on a monthly basis.
	On a daily basis, a departmental clerk reviews reconciling items identified in the comparison of the ABC report with the data feed from user entities.
The party responsible for performing the control	The security manager reviews . . .
	An input processing clerk compares . . .
The nature of the activity that is performed	The system compares the name of the user entity employee requesting access to the system with approved user information submitted by authorized user entity personnel.
	Service organization department managers review the list of service organization personnel who have access to the system for appropriateness of access on a monthly basis and evidence this review with a sign-off.
The subject matter to which the control is applied	Program changes are reviewed by. . . .

3.05 In determining whether the description of the service organization's system is fairly presented, the service auditor compares his or her understanding of the service provided and the system through which it is provided with the description of the service organization's system, as they relate to the trust services principle(s) being reported on. The description is considered fairly presented if it includes the information required by paragraphs 1.33–.34 of this guide, does not omit or distort information relevant to users, and objectively describes what actually occurs at the service organization.

3.06 The description is not fairly presented if it states or implies that system elements exist that do not exist, if it states or implies that controls are being performed when they are not being performed, or if it inadvertently or intentionally omits or distorts relevant system information.

3.07   Additionally, a description that is fairly presented should not contain statements that cannot be objectively evaluated. For example, describing a service organization as being the "world's best" or "most respected in the industry" is subjective and, therefore, would not be appropriate for inclusion in a description of the service organization's system.

3.08   As part of the service auditor's evaluation of whether the description materially omits information relevant to users, the service auditor determines whether the description addresses all the major aspects of the system within the scope of the engagement. An example of an omission would be failing to include in the description significant aspects of the processing performed at another location that is included in the scope of the engagement.

3.09   A service organization may have controls that it considers to be outside the boundaries of the system, such as controls related to the conversion of new user entities to the service organization's systems. To avoid misunderstanding by users, the service auditor considers whether the description clearly delineates the boundaries of the system that are included in the scope of the engagement.

3.10   When performing a type 2 engagement, the service auditor should inquire about changes in the service organization's system, such as changes in controls that were implemented during the period covered by the service auditor's report. (If the report addresses the privacy principle, this would include changes in the service organization's privacy practices.) If the service auditor believes that the changes would be considered significant by users, the service auditor should determine whether the changes have been included in the description of the service organization's system at an appropriate level of detail, including the date the change occurred and how the system differed before and after the change. If the changes relate to privacy practices, they would be included in the description of the service organization's system or the service organization's statement of privacy practices. If management has not included such changes in the description, the service auditor should ask management to amend the description to include this information. If management refuses to include this information in the description, the service auditor considers the effect of such changes on his or her conclusions regarding the fairness of the presentation of management's description of the service organization's system and the service auditor's report.

3.11   In evaluating which aspects of the service organization's system are relevant and should be included in the description of the service organization's system, the service auditor considers the common information needs of the broad range of users for whom the report is intended.

3.12   Paragraphs 1.33–.34 of this guide present the information to be included in management's description of the service organization's system. Paragraph 1.33(a)(x) requires the description to include aspects of the service organization's internal control other than its control activities if they are relevant to meeting the applicable trust services criteria (for example, aspects of the control environment). If these aspects relate to meeting a specific criterion, they should be included in the description of the specific controls designed to meet that criterion.

Evaluating Whether Controls Have Been Implemented

3.13 To be fairly presented, the description of the service organization's system should include only controls that have been implemented. Controls that have been implemented have been placed in operation versus existing only in the description. The service auditor should determine whether the controls included in management's description of the service organization's system have been implemented by performing inquiry in combination with other procedures. Such other procedures may include observation, inspection of records and other documentation of the manner in which the service organization's system operates and controls are applied, and reperformance of the control.

3.14 The service auditor's procedures to determine whether the controls included in the description have been implemented may be similar to, and performed in conjunction with, procedures to obtain an understanding of the system and the system's boundaries. For example, when performing a walkthrough to verify the service auditor's understanding of the design of controls, the service auditor may also determine whether controls have been implemented as stated in the description of the service organization's system. Performing a walkthrough entails asking relevant members of the service organization's management and staff to describe and demonstrate their actions in performing a procedure. In performing a walkthrough, the service auditor follows a system, event, or activity from origination through the service organization's processes, including its information systems, until its final disposition, using the same documents and IT that service organization personnel use. Walkthrough procedures usually include a combination of inquiry; observation; inspection of relevant documentation (that is, corroboration); and reperformance of controls. It may be helpful to use flowcharts, questionnaires, or decision tables to facilitate understanding the design of the controls.

3.15 If the service auditor determines that certain controls identified in management's description have not been implemented, the service auditor should ask management of the service organization to delete those controls from the description. The service auditor considers only controls that have been implemented when assessing the suitability of the design and operating effectiveness of controls. Paragraph 4.22 of this guide presents an illustrative explanatory paragraph that would be added to the service auditor's report when the description includes controls that have not been implemented.

Other Information in the Description That Is Not Covered by the Service Auditor's Report

3.16 A service organization may wish to provide report users with information, other than the information required by paragraphs 1.33–.34 of this guide, that will not be covered by the service auditor's report. Examples of such information are pending changes to the system and regulatory matters. Such other information should be distinguished from the service organization's description of its system by excluding the information from the description. If the other information is attached to the description or included in a document that contains the description of the service organization's system and the service auditor's report, the other information should be differentiated from the information covered by the service auditor's report, for example, through the use of a title such as "Other Information Provided by Example Service Organization That Is Not Covered by the Service Auditor's Report."

3.17 When other information that is not covered by the service auditor's report is attached to the description or included in a document containing the description and the service auditor's report, the service auditor should apply the requirements and guidance in paragraph .92 of AT section 101, *Attest Engagements* (AICPA, *Professional Standards*), which requires the service auditor to read the other information and identify any material inconsistencies, such as an apparent misstatement of fact. Ordinarily, the service auditor would discuss such inconsistencies with management of the service organization, and if management refuses to correct the information, the service auditor should determine which of the actions described in paragraphs .92–.94 of AT section 101 are appropriate.

3.18 The service auditor may wish to emphasize that the other information is not a part of the description of the service organization's system and is not covered by the service auditor's report. In these instances, the service auditor may include an explanatory paragraph in the report describing the other information and stating that the service auditor's report does not address the other information. Paragraph 4.27 of this guide presents an example of such a paragraph.

Materiality Relating to the Fair Presentation of the Description

3.19 The service auditor should consider materiality when evaluating the fair presentation of the description of the service organization's system. Materiality in this context primarily relates to qualitative factors, such as whether significant aspects of the system and processing have been included in the description or whether relevant information has been omitted or distorted.

3.20 The following are some examples of how the service auditor might consider materiality when evaluating whether the description of a service organization's system is fairly presented:

- Example Service Organization uses a subservice organization to perform all of its back-office functions and elects to use the carve-out method of presentation. Management's description of the service organization's system includes information about the nature of the services provided by the subservice organization and describes the service organization's monitoring and other controls that the service organization implements with respect to the processing performed by the subservice organization. In this example, the description of the service organization's system should include such information because it is likely to be relevant to users and, therefore, would be considered material to the description.

- A service auditor is reporting on Example Service Organization's controls related to the security principle. Example Service Organization uses a separate facility for its off-site storage of backup tapes. Data written to the backup tapes is encrypted, and Example Service Organization's description includes information about its controls over the encryption of the information. The description does not include information about controls over physical access to the separate facility. Controls over physical access would be intended to meet the following trust services criterion: procedures exist to restrict physical access to the defined system, including, but not limited to, facilities; backup media; and other system components, such as firewalls, routers, and servers. In this example, such an omission is not likely to be material to users because controls over the encryption of the tapes prevent unauthorized access to the information and compensate for the omission of controls over physical access to the facility.

Complementary User-Entity Controls

3.21 A service organization may design its services with the assumption that certain controls will be implemented by the user entities. If such complementary user-entity controls are necessary to meet certain applicable trust services criteria, the service auditor evaluates whether the service organization's description adequately describes the complementary user-entity controls and their importance in meeting the applicable trust services criteria to which they relate.

3.22 To evaluate whether complementary user-entity controls included in the description are adequately described, the service auditor compares the information in the description with documents such as contracts with user entities and system or procedure manuals and makes inquiries of service organization personnel to gain an understanding of the user entities' responsibilities for achieving the applicable trust services criteria and whether those responsibilities are appropriately described in the description.

3.23 For example, if the service organization manages logical security for the user entities and provides access to its system based on user-entity authorization, the following trust services criterion could not be met without the implementation of controls at the user entities because access authorization rests with them: procedures exist to restrict logical access to the defined system, including, but not limited to, registration and authorization of new users. Accordingly, in addition to describing the relevant controls performed by the service organization, the description would include information, such as the following, alerting user entities to the need for a complementary user-entity control: user entities are responsible for implementing controls over the authorization of access to the system by employees of the user entity and for communicating to the service organization user registration and access information in a timely manner.

Subservice Organizations

3.24 Management of the service organization should determine whether controls over the functions performed by an organization from which it has contracted services (a vendor) are needed to meet one of more of the trust services criteria or are otherwise relevant to the fair presentation of the description of the service organization's system. If so, the vendor is considered a subservice organization, and the service organization's description of its system should include, depending on whether the inclusive or carve-out method is used, the information set forth in paragraphs 3.26 and 3.29. For each subservice organization, the service organization determines whether to use the inclusive method of presentation, as described in paragraphs 3.26–.28, or the carve-out method of presentation, as described in paragraph 3.29. The service auditor should obtain an understanding of the significant vendors whose services affect the service organization's system and assess whether management has made an appropriate determination about whether these vendors are subservice organizations. Paragraphs 4.37–.39 of this guide present illustrative report paragraphs marked to show the changes that would be made to those paragraphs when using the carve-out method. (The illustrative report paragraphs in paragraph 4.39 of this guide show the changes that would be made to the report if the service organization uses the carve-out method, and the service auditor is disclaiming an opinion.) Paragraph 4.40 of this guide presents an illustrative report marked to show the changes that would be made to the report when the inclusive method is used.

3.25 In evaluating services provided by a vendor, the service organization should assess whether controls at the service organization alone or the service organization's monitoring of the effectiveness of controls at the vendor enable the applicable trust services criteria affected by those services to be met. Examples of monitoring the effectiveness of a vendor's controls include tests of the vendor's controls performed by the service organization's internal audit function, review and approval of vendor output, periodic visits to the vendor and assessments, and review of reports on attestation engagements that address the vendor's services and controls. In these instances, the service organization does not need to treat the vendor as a subservice organization, omits from the description information about controls at the vendor, and omits any description of the effect the vendor's controls may have on meeting the applicable trust services criteria. When a service organization has determined that its controls alone meet the applicable trust services criteria or that its monitoring of the vendor's controls is sufficient to meet the related criteria, the service auditor evaluates this determination as part of the evaluation of the suitability of the design of the controls in meeting the applicable trust services criteria and tests the operating effectiveness of such controls or the monitoring performed by the subservice organization.

3.26 For the purposes of this guide, under the inclusive method, the relevant aspects of the subservice organization's infrastructure, software, people, procedures, and data are to be considered a part of the service organization's system and would be included in the description of the service organization's system. Although these relevant aspects would be considered a part of the service organization's system, the portions of the system that are attributable to the subservice organization should be separately identified.

3.27 When the inclusive method is used, the guidance set forth in this guide also applies to the services provided by the subservice organization to the extent they affect the service organization's ability to meet the applicable trust services criteria, including the following:

- Obtaining acknowledgement and acceptance of responsibility for the matters in paragraph 2.13 of this guide from management of the subservice organization

- Obtaining an understanding of the portion of the system provided by the subservice organization

- Obtaining and evaluating evidence about the fairness of the presentation of the description for the portions of the system provided by the subservice organization

- Obtaining evidence about whether the described controls have been implemented at the subservice organization

- Evaluating the suitability of the design of controls at the subservice organization

- For a type 2 report, obtaining evidence of the operating effectiveness of controls at the subservice organization

- Obtaining evidence of the subservice organization's compliance with the privacy commitments it has made to the service organization, if applicable

- For a type 2 report, obtaining a written assertion addressing the matters in paragraph 1.16(a)(ii)(1)–(4) of this guide that are relevant to the services provided by the subservice organization, and for a type 1 report, the matters in paragraph 1.16(b)(ii)(1)–(2) of this guide

- Obtaining written representations about the matters in paragraph 3.90 that are relevant to the services provided by the subservice organization

3.28 When the inclusive method is used, the service auditor should

- evaluate whether the description of the service organization's system, including the relevant aspects of the system provided by the subservice organization, is fairly presented.

- evaluate the suitability of the design of the controls at the subservice organization.

- for a type 2 report, perform tests of the operating effectiveness of those controls.

- when the report addresses the privacy principle, test the subservice organization's compliance with the commitments in the service organization's statement of privacy practices.

3.29 If the service organization uses the carve-out method to present a subservice organization, the description of the service organization's system identifies the following:

- The nature of the services provided by the subservice organization

- If the description addresses the privacy principle, any aspects of the personal information life cycle for which responsibility has been delegated to the subservice organization, if applicable

- Each of the applicable trust services criteria that are intended to be met by controls at the subservice organization alone or in combination with controls at the service organization

- The types of controls expected to be implemented at carved-out subservice organizations that are necessary to meet the applicable trust services criteria, either alone or in combination with controls at the service organization

- If the description addresses the privacy principle, the types of activities that the subservice organization would need to perform to comply with the service organization's privacy commitments

The description of the service organization's system and the service auditor's engagement exclude all other aspects of the subservice organization's infrastructure, software, people, procedures, and data relevant to the services provided (see additional considerations in paragraphs 3.37–.39).

3.30 A service organization may use multiple subservice organizations and prepare its description using the carve-out method of presentation for one or more subservice organizations and the inclusive method of presentation for others.

3.31 Paragraph 4.23 of this guide presents an illustrative explanatory paragraph that would be added to the service auditor's report when the service organization uses a subservice organization but refuses to disclose that fact and the functions that the subservice organization performs.

Changes in the Scope of the Engagement

3.32 Management of the service organization may request a change in the scope of the engagement prior to the completion of the engagement (for example, a change in the trust services principles to be covered, the services that the service organization provides [for example discontinuing a particular service], the boundaries of the service organization's system, the components of the system, or the use of the inclusive or carve-out method for subservice organizations). When management requests such a change in scope, the service auditor should be satisfied, before agreeing to the change, that a reasonable justification for the change exists. Reasonable justification may include the following:

- Changes in the needs of users of the reports
- Identification of additional system components or expansion of the boundaries of the system to be included in the description to improve the fairness of the presentation of the description
- Determination that certain system components are not relevant to the services provided
- Determination that certain services are not relevant to users
- The inability to arrange for the service auditor's access to a subservice organization

Generally, increases in the scope of the engagement are likely to have a reasonable justification. A request to decrease the scope of the engagement may not have a reasonable justification if, for example, the request is made

- to exclude portions of the system because of the likelihood that the service auditor's opinion would be modified with respect to those portions of the system.
- to prevent the disclosure of deviations identified at a subservice organization by requesting a change from the inclusive method to the carve-out method.

3.33 When a service auditor determines that a request to change the scope of an engagement derives from intent by a responsible party (for example, management of the service organization or a subservice organization) to conceal information relevant to the user, such as deficiencies in the operating effectiveness of a control, the service auditor should take appropriate action, which may include adding an explanatory paragraph to his or her report, disclaiming an opinion, or withdrawing from the engagement. If the request to change the scope of the engagement derives from refusal by management of the subservice organization to provide a written assertion or written representations, after having agreed to do so, the service auditor should disclaim an opinion due to the service auditor's inability to obtain evidence regarding the suitability of the design and operating effectiveness of controls at the subservice organization.

Evaluating the Suitability of the Design of Controls

3.34 A control is suitably designed if, individually or in combination with other controls, it would, when complied with satisfactorily, provide reasonable assurance that the applicable trust services criteria would be met. The trust services criteria for a SOC 2 engagement are included in appendix B, "Trust Services Principles and Criteria for Security, Availability, Processing Integrity, Confidentiality, and Privacy," of this guide. In assessing whether controls are suitably designed, the service auditor considers the following:

- The events and circumstances that might prevent the applicable trust services criteria from being met
- Whether the controls, if operating effectively, would prevent, or detect and correct, those events and circumstances

3.35 The service auditor uses the information and evidence obtained in determining whether the description of the service organization's system is fairly presented to evaluate the suitability of the design of controls and obtains additional evidence by performing procedures that may include the following:

- Inquiry of service organization personnel regarding the operation of controls and the types of errors that occur
- Inspection of documents produced by the system
- Performing additional walkthroughs of control activity-related policies and procedures
- Reading system documentation

3.36 A control may meet more than one criterion or multiple controls may be needed to meet a single criterion. If a combination of controls is needed to meet one or more criteria, the service auditor considers the combination of controls jointly.

3.37 If the service organization uses the carve-out method for a subservice organization, the service auditor also evaluates whether the types of controls expected to be implemented at the carved-out subservice organization that are necessary to meet specified applicable trust services criteria, either alone or in combination with controls at the service organization, would, if operating effectively, meet the specified applicable trust services criteria. The service auditor also considers whether evidence exists that the subservice organization is aware of the service organization's requirements with regard to these types of controls and whether there is any evidence that weaknesses exist in the suitability of the design or operating effectiveness of controls at the subservice organization. Examples of procedures that may be performed to obtain such evidence include the following:

- Reading contracts with the subservice organization to determine if they identify the types of controls expected to be implemented at the subservice organization
- Obtaining an understanding of the procedures in place at the service organization to evaluate and monitor the implementation, suitability of design, and operating effectiveness of the controls at the subservice organization (for example, evaluation of a service

auditor's report on the description of the subservice organizat
system prepared using this guide or testing performed at the subservice organization by service organization personnel)

- Obtaining and evaluating a type 2 report on the subservice organization's system prepared using this guide

3.38 The service auditor considers whether the services provided by the
subservice organization are of such a nature that the use of the carve-out
method prevents the description from being fairly presented and causes the
description to be misleading to users. The service auditor considers the extent
to which

- important system functions necessary for understanding the system are performed by the subservice organization.
- controls at the subservice organization are necessary to meet the
applicable trust services criteria.
- the service organization's compliance with the commitments in
its statement of privacy practices is dependent on the subservice
organization's compliance with those commitments.

Factors to consider in making this determination include the following:

- The number of applicable trust services criteria that would not
be met if the types of controls expected to be implemented at the
carved-out subservice organization that are necessary to meet the
criteria, either alone or in combination with controls at the service
organization, were not implemented
- The complexity of the services and the types of controls that would
be expected to be implemented by the subservice organization
- The complexity of the interaction of the service organization and
subservice organization.
- The ability of the service auditor to obtain sufficient appropriate
evidence regarding controls at the service organization affected by
controls at the carved-out subservice organization.

3.39 If the service auditor determines that the effect of the types of controls expected to be implemented at the subservice organization in meeting
the applicable trust services criteria is pervasive, and the description of the
service organization's system when presented using the carve-out method is
misleading to users, the service auditor may

- suggest to management that the scope of the engagement be
changed to the inclusive method.
- add additional material to the scope paragraph of the service auditor's report explaining the nature and extent of the effect of the
subservice organization on the service organization (for example,
the nature and extent of the service organization's dependence on
the subservice organization).
- add a paragraph to the service auditor's report disclaiming an
opinion on the suitability of the design and operating effectiveness
of controls at the subservice organization that are necessary, in
combination with controls at the service organization, to meet the
specified applicable trust services criteria, due to the service auditor's inability to obtain sufficient appropriate evidence regarding

the suitability of the design and operating effectiveness of controls at the subservice organization.

- disclaim an opinion on all of the matters covered by the service auditor's report.

Paragraph 4.39 of this guide presents an explanatory paragraph that would be added to the service auditor's report when disclaiming an opinion in these circumstances, as well as the disclaimer language that replaces the opinion paragraph.

3.40 The service auditor should consider materiality with respect to the suitability of the design of controls primarily by considering qualitative factors, such as whether the controls have the ability, as designed, to provide reasonable assurance that the applicable trust services criteria would be met, and quantitative factors, such as the maximum rate of control failure that is acceptable to the service organization and whether that rate is less than the service auditor's tolerable rate of deviation.

3.41 In evaluating the suitability of the design of controls, the service auditor considers the effect of the control environment and other components of the service organization's internal control on the ability of the controls to meet the applicable trust services criteria.

3.42 A service organization's controls may vary, depending on the nature of the information processed or the manner in which it is transmitted. For example, user entities may submit information to a service organization by mail, phone, fax, or Internet. Controls over the capture of that information may vary depending on the method by which the information is submitted. In order for a specified criterion to be met, the service organization's controls would need to address all the significant variations.

3.43 A service organization that has multiple controls that each independently meet a particular criterion may choose to include only one of the controls in the description. If the service auditor determines that the described control is not suitably designed to meet a particular criterion and becomes aware of one or more other controls that are suitably designed to meet the criterion, the service auditor should ask management to revise the description to include the additional control(s).

3.44 After performing the procedures and considering the guidance in paragraphs 3.34–.43, the service auditor considers whether the controls have the ability, as designed, to provide reasonable assurance that the applicable trust services criteria are met.

3.45 Paragraphs 4.29–4.30 and 4.32 of this guide present illustrative explanatory paragraphs that would be added to the service auditor's report when the service auditor determines that controls are not suitably designed to meet one or more of the applicable trust services criteria.

Obtaining Evidence Regarding the Operating Effectiveness of Controls in a Type 2 Engagement

3.46 When performing a type 2 engagement, the service auditor should test the operating effectiveness of the controls stated in management's description of the service organization's system that are necessary to meet the applicable trust services criteria throughout the period covered by the service auditor's report. The service auditor is responsible for determining the nature, timing, and extent of the procedures to be performed in evaluating whether the controls are operating effectively.

3.47 From the viewpoint of the service auditor, a control is operating effectively if it functions as intended throughout the period. When the service organization uses the inclusive method, the service auditor considers the controls at both the service organization and subservice organization.

3.48 A control may be designed to address an identified risk on its own or may function in combination with another control. For example, when a supervisor reviews and approves a user's credentials prior to providing the user with access to the system, the manual control (review and approval of the user's credentials) may be complemented by a system's application control requiring that a supervisor acknowledge his or her review and approval by entering a sign-off in the system prior to providing access to the system. In this instance, both the manual and automated controls would be tested by the service auditor because the two controls are dependent on one another.

3.49 The service auditor should consider materiality when evaluating whether controls are operating with sufficient effectiveness to meet the applicable trust services criteria. Materiality with respect to the operating effectiveness of controls includes the consideration of the following:

- Quantitative factors, such as the tolerable rate of deviation and the observed rate of deviation. (In this guide, the *tolerable rate of deviation* is the maximum rate of deviations in the operation of the prescribed control that the service auditor is willing to accept without modifying the opinion relating to one or more applicable trust services criteria.)
- Qualitative factors (for example, the nature and cause of any identified deviations).

3.50 If the service organization implemented changes to its controls during the period covered by the service auditor's report, and the superseded controls could be relevant to meeting one or more applicable trust services criteria during a portion of the period covered by the service auditor's report, the superseded controls should be included in the population of controls to be tested. If the service organization has used the inclusive method, the service auditor considers changes to controls at both the service organization and subservice organization.

Designing and Performing Tests of Controls

3.51 When determining the nature, timing, and extent of tests of controls to be performed to obtain evidence of the operating effectiveness of controls, the service auditor considers the type of evidence that can be obtained about the performance of the control and how long that evidence will be available. The service auditor also considers whether a particular control is designed to meet one or more criteria on its own or in combination with other controls. If a combination of controls is necessary to meet a given criteria, those controls are considered together, and deviations are evaluated together. The service auditor also considers the risk that the control will not operate effectively.

3.52 The service organization's control environment or other components of internal control related to the service provided to user entities may enhance or mitigate the effectiveness of specific controls. If the service auditor determines that certain aspects of the control environment or other components of internal control are not effective, the service auditor generally would obtain more convincing evidence of the operating effectiveness of the specific controls to determine whether the related trust services criteria have been met. In some situations, the service auditor may conclude that controls are not operating effectively to meet certain related trust services criteria because of deficiencies in the control environment or other components of internal control.

3.53 For example, consider a service organization that determines bonuses based on zero processing errors. In this environment, service organization personnel may be tempted to suppress the reporting of errors in order to receive bonuses. The service auditor may decide to increase the testing of controls that prevent, or detect and correct, errors in system processing (for example, reconciliations of input to output designed to identify exceptions) or, perhaps, may even test the entire population to determine whether controls are operating effectively to meet the applicable trust services criteria.

Nature of Tests of Controls

3.54 When designing and performing tests of controls, the service auditor

- a. makes inquiries and performs other procedures to obtain evidence about the following:
  - i. How the control was applied. (Was the control performed as designed?)
  - ii. The consistency with which the control was applied throughout the period.
  - iii. By whom or by what means the control was applied. (Is the control automated or manual? Has there been high turnover in the position, and is the control being performed by an inexperienced person?)
- b. determines whether the controls to be tested depend on other controls and, if so, whether it is necessary to obtain evidence supporting the operating effectiveness of those other controls.
- c. determines an effective method for selecting the items to be tested to meet the objectives of the procedure.

3.55 The other procedures that the service auditor should perform in combination with inquiry to obtain evidence about the operating effectiveness of controls include the following:

- Observation of the application of the control
- Inspection of documents, reports, or electronic files that contain evidence of the performance of the controls, such as system log files
- Reperformance of the control

3.56 Inquiry alone usually does not provide sufficient appropriate evidence of the operating effectiveness of controls. Some tests of controls provide more convincing evidence of the operating effectiveness of controls than others. Performing inquiry combined with inspection or reperformance ordinarily provides more convincing evidence than performing inquiry and observation.

3.57 Evidence of the operating effectiveness of controls may be lost, misplaced, or inadvertently deleted by the service organization. In such instances, the service auditor determines whether other evidence of the operating effectiveness of the control exists and whether the results of tests of the other evidence would provide sufficient appropriate evidence. If not, the service auditor should modify the report. Paragraph 4.34 of this guide presents an illustrative explanatory paragraph that would be added to the service auditor's report when a scope limitation exists that prevents the service auditor from obtaining evidence about the operating effectiveness of controls.

3.58 When information produced by the service organization's information system is provided to the service auditor as a source for testing, the service auditor should obtain evidence about the validity, completeness, and accuracy of that information. For example, the service organization might provide the service auditor with a quarterly system-generated report of user access to the system that is reviewed by management for appropriateness of access based on assigned job responsibilities. In testing management's review, the service auditor evaluates whether the report is complete and accurate, based on the user access rules for the system.

Testing Controls at an Interim Date

3.59 The service auditor may perform tests of controls at interim dates, at the end of the examination period, or after the examination period. The following are some relevant factors to be considered when determining the timing of tests of controls:

- The nature of the controls
- The period of time during which the information will be available (for example, electronic files may be overwritten after a period of time or hard copy records may not be retained)
- Whether testing requires direct observation of a procedure that is only performed at certain times during the examination period
- Whether the control leaves evidence of its operation and, if not, whether the control must be tested through observation

3.60 Performing procedures at an interim date may assist management of the service organization in identifying deficiencies in the design or operating effectiveness of controls at an early stage in the examination and provides the service organization with an opportunity to correct the deficiencies for the remainder of the examination period. Paragraph 4.32 of this guide contains an illustrative paragraph that would be added to the service auditor's report if the service auditor concludes that controls were not suitably designed to meet an applicable trust services criterion during a portion of the period under examination.

3.61 When the service auditor performs tests of the operating effectiveness of controls at an interim period, the service auditor should determine what additional testing is necessary for the remaining period.

Extent of Tests of Controls

3.62 The service auditor should design and perform tests of controls to obtain sufficient appropriate evidence that the controls are operating effectively throughout the period to meet the applicable trust services criteria. Relevant factors in determining the extent of tests of controls include the following:

- The nature of the controls
- The frequency of the performance of the control during the period (for example, daily management review of open incidents versus monthly review of closed incidents to identify ongoing problems)
- The relevance and reliability of the evidence that can be obtained to support the conclusion that the controls are operating effectively to meet the applicable trust services criteria
- The extent to which audit evidence is obtained from tests of other controls designed to meet the same criterion
- The service organization's maximum acceptable rate of control failure
- The service auditor's tolerable rate of deviation in the operating effectiveness of the control

3.63 If the control operates frequently, the service auditor should consider using audit sampling to obtain reasonable assurance about the operating effectiveness of the control. If the control is applied on a periodic basis (for example, a monthly reconciliation of input to output), the service auditor should consider guidance appropriate for testing smaller populations. Refer further to AU section 350, *Audit Sampling* (AICPA, *Professional Standards*), and the Audit Guide *Audit Sampling*.

3.64 The service auditor should test the operating effectiveness of the control in effect throughout the period covered by the report and determine whether the control has operated frequently enough to be assessed as operating effectively. For example, if a report covers a period of six months, and a control operates only annually, the service auditor may be unable to test the operating effectiveness of the control within the period. The shorter the test period, the greater the risk that certain controls may not have operated during the period and that the service auditor will be unable to perform sufficient testing and obtain sufficient evidence to express an opinion on the operating effectiveness of those controls.

3.65 Generally, evidence obtained in prior engagements about the satisfactory operation of controls in prior periods does not provide a basis for a reduction in testing in the current examination period, even if it is supplemented with evidence obtained during the current period. If the service auditor plans to use evidence about the operating effectiveness of controls obtained in prior engagements, the service auditor should adapt and apply the guidance in paragraph .40 of AU section 318, *Performing Audit Procedures in Response to Assessed Risks and Evaluating the Audit Evidence Obtained* (AICPA, *Professional Standards*), which requires the service auditor to obtain evidence about whether changes in those specific controls have occurred subsequent to the prior engagement by a combination of observation, inquiry, and inspection to confirm the understanding of those specific controls. Paragraph .40 of AU section 318 refers to the guidance in paragraph .24 of AU section 326, *Audit Evidence* (AICPA, *Professional Standards*), which states that the service auditor should perform procedures to establish the continuing relevance of evidence obtained in prior periods when the service auditor plans to use such evidence in the current period. For example, in performing the prior examination, the service auditor may have determined that an automated control was functioning as intended.

The service auditor should obtain evidence to determine whether changes to the automated control have been made that affect its continued effective functioning (for example, through inquiries of management and the inspection of logs to indicate whether controls have been changed). Consideration of evidence about these changes may support either increasing or decreasing the expected evidence to be obtained in the current period about the operating effectiveness of the controls.

3.66 If the service auditor intends to use evidence of the operating effectiveness of controls that was obtained in prior periods, and those controls have changed since they were last tested, the service auditor should perform additional tests of the operating effectiveness of such controls in the current period. Changes may affect the relevance of the evidence obtained in prior periods such that it may no longer be relevant. For example, changes in a system that enable the service organization to receive a new report from the system probably do not affect the relevance of prior period evidence; however, a change that causes data to be accumulated or calculated differently does affect it.

3.67 If the service auditor identified deviations in the operation of a control in a prior year, the service auditor may decide to increase the extent of testing in the current period. For example, if the opinion in the prior year's service auditor's report was qualified because of deviations in controls over the authorization of user access, the service auditor may decide to increase the number of items tested in the current examination period. This would be the case if the design or operation of the control had not been corrected in the current year, which may result in the same kinds of deviations, or if a new control had been implemented (a new control may not have been thoroughly tested and may have unexpected deficiencies in design or operating effectiveness, increasing the risk that the controls would not have operated effectively).

3.68 Generally, IT processing is inherently consistent; therefore, the service auditor may be able to limit the testing to one or a few instances of the control operation. An automated control should function consistently, unless the program, including the tables, files, or other permanent data used by the program, is changed. Once the service auditor determines that an automated control is functioning as intended, which could be determined at the time the control is initially implemented or at some other date, the service auditor should perform tests to determine that the control continues to function effectively. Such tests might include determining that changes to the program are not made without being subject to the appropriate program change controls, that the authorized version of the program is used for processing transactions, and that other relevant IT general controls are effective.

3.69 A control may be designed to address an identified risk on its own or may function in combination with another control. Often, the effectiveness of the control will depend on both manual and automated procedures. For example, management's follow-up of system-identified security access violation events is dependent on the proper configuration and functioning of the security monitoring software.

Selecting Items to Be Tested

3.70 When determining the extent of tests of controls and whether sampling is appropriate, the service auditor should consider the characteristics of the population of the controls to be tested, including the nature of the controls, the frequency of their application, and the expected deviation rate. AU section 350 addresses planning, performing, and evaluating audit samples. If the service auditor determines that sampling is appropriate, the service auditor should apply the requirements in paragraphs .31–.43 of AU section 350 that address sampling in tests of controls. Paragraphs .01–.14 and .45–.46 of AU section 350 provide additional guidance regarding the principles underlying those paragraphs.

Controls Included in the Description That Are Not Tested

3.71 There may be situations in which the service auditor is unable to test controls related to certain applicable trust services criteria because there were no instances of the control operating during the examination period. In these situations, the service auditor's tests should identify the applicable trust services criteria for which tests of controls have not been performed and the reasons why they have not been performed.

Testing Changes to Controls

3.72 If the service organization makes changes to controls during the period that are relevant to meeting the applicable trust services criteria stated in the description, and the service auditor believes the changes would be considered significant by users, the service auditor should test the superseded controls before the change and test the new controls after the change for the period they were in effect. For example, during the period June 1, 20X0, to May 31, 20X1, Example Service Organization decided to automate a control that was previously performed manually. The service organization automated the control on December 15, 20X0. The service auditor tests the manual control for the period June 1, 20X0, to December 14, 20X0, considering the nature and frequency of the performance of the control, and then tests the automated control for the period December 15, 20X0, to May 31, 20X1, considering the guidance in paragraph 3.62 and the nature and frequency of the performance of each control. If the service auditor cannot test the superseded controls, the service auditor would disclose that fact in the description of tests and results and determine the effect on the service auditor's report.

Testing Compliance With Privacy Commitments

3.73 In a type 2 engagement that addresses the privacy principle, in addition to expressing an opinion on the design and operating effectiveness of controls, the service auditor also expresses an opinion on whether the service organization complied with the commitments in its statement of privacy practices (privacy commitments). Information obtained from the service auditor's assessment of the design and operating effectiveness of controls related to privacy contributes to his or her evaluation of the risk of material noncompliance with the service organization's privacy commitments, which includes both intentional and unintentional material noncompliance. The service auditor uses this information as part, but not all, of the reasonable basis for his or her opinion regarding the service organization's compliance with its privacy commitments.

3.74 Based on the assessment of the controls that address the trust services privacy criteria, the service auditor determines the extent to which he or she needs to perform tests to detect material noncompliance with the privacy commitments. Accordingly, the service auditor may alter the nature, timing, and extent of tests performed, based on the assessments and tests of the controls.

3.75 In an engagement in which the service auditor reports on an entity's compliance with its privacy commitments, the service auditor's consideration of materiality is affected by (*a*) the nature of the requirements in the statement of privacy practices; (*b*) the nature and frequency of identified noncompliance, with appropriate consideration of sampling risk; and (*c*) qualitative considerations, including the needs and expectations of the report users.

3.76 The service auditor should apply procedures to provide reasonable assurance of detecting material noncompliance. Determining these procedures and evaluating the sufficiency of the evidence obtained are matters of professional judgment. When exercising such judgment, the service auditor should consider the guidance in AU section 350 and paragraphs .51–.54 of AT section 101.

3.77 The following example illustrates how a service auditor might consider the foregoing in planning tests of compliance with privacy commitments:

> A service organization's statement of privacy practices contains a commitment not to share personal information obtained from users with other users. Based on the service auditor's evaluation and tests, the service organization's controls over access to personal information are effective in meeting the relevant criteria and in preventing one user's employees from accessing personal information provided by any other user. To test compliance with this commitment, the service auditor compares a daily log of all accesses to personal information with a list, furnished by the user entity, of the names of user-entity employees authorized to access such information. Because the access controls related to this commitment were effective, the service auditor determined that it would only be necessary to perform this test on a limited number of daily logs throughout the period. Had the controls not been as effective or had the service auditor identified deviations while testing controls, the number of daily logs tested for compliance would need to be greater.

Using the Work of the Internal Audit Function

3.78 Paragraphs 2.16–.22 of this guide discuss the service auditor's responsibilities for the following:

- Obtaining an understanding of the responsibilities and activities of the service organization's internal audit function

- Determining whether work performed by the internal audit function is adequate for the service auditor's purposes

- Determining the planned effect of that work on the service auditor's procedures

3.79 In order for a service auditor to use specific work of the internal audit function, the service auditor should evaluate and perform procedures on that work to determine whether it is adequate for the service auditor's purposes by evaluating whether

a. the work was performed by members of the internal audit function having adequate technical training and proficiency;

b. the work was properly supervised, reviewed, and documented;

c. sufficient appropriate evidence was obtained to enable the internal audit function to draw reasonable conclusions;

d. conclusions reached are appropriate in the circumstances, and any reports prepared by the internal audit function are consistent with the results of the work performed; and

e. exceptions relevant to the engagement or unusual matters disclosed by the internal audit function are properly resolved.

3.80   The nature, timing, and extent of the service auditor's procedures performed on specific work of the internal auditor function will depend on the service auditor's assessment of the significance of that work to the service auditor's conclusions (for example, the significance of the risks that the controls are intended to mitigate); the evaluation of the internal audit function; and the evaluation of the specific work of the internal audit function. Such procedures may include the following:

- Examination of items already examined by the internal audit function

- Examination of other similar items

- Observation of procedures performed by the internal audit function

3.81   When the internal audit function provides direct assistance to the service auditor, as described in paragraphs 2.16 and 4.10 of this guide, the service auditor should

- inform the internal auditors of their responsibilities; the objectives of the procedures they are to perform; and matters that may affect the nature, timing, and extent of the audit procedures.

- supervise, review, evaluate, and test the work performed by the internal auditors to the extent appropriate in the circumstances.

Evaluating the Results of Tests

3.82   The service auditor should evaluate the results of tests of controls and, if the report addresses the privacy principle, the results of tests of compliance with the service organization's commitments in its statement of privacy practices. In evaluating the results of tests, the service auditor investigates the nature and cause of any identified deviations and determines whether

- identified deviations are within the tolerable rate of deviation and are acceptable. If so, the testing that has been performed provides an appropriate basis for concluding that the control operated effectively throughout the specified period.

- additional testing of the same control or other controls designed to meet the same criterion is necessary to reach a conclusion about whether the controls related to the criterion operated effectively throughout the specified period.

- the testing that has been performed provides an appropriate basis for concluding that the control did not operate effectively throughout the specified period.

3.83 If the service auditor is unable to apply the planned testing procedures or appropriate alternative procedures to selected items, the service auditor considers the reasons for this limitation and ordinarily considers those selected items to be deviations from the prescribed policy or procedure for the purpose of evaluating the sample.

3.84 The service auditor evaluates deficiencies related to the control environment or other components of the service organization's internal control and determines the effect on the service auditor's opinion. For example, the service auditor considers how deficiencies in the control environment would alter the nature, timing, and extent of his or her procedures. In certain circumstances, identified deficiencies may be so pervasive that they may prevent controls from meeting one or more of the applicable trust services criteria, which may result in a qualified or an adverse opinion.

3.85 If the service auditor becomes aware of deviations that have resulted from intentional acts by service organization personnel, incidents of noncompliance with laws and regulations, or other adverse events not prevented or detected by a control that may affect one or more user entities, the service auditor should determine whether this information should be communicated to affected user entities and whether this communication has occurred. If the information has not been communicated, and management of the service organization is unwilling to do so, the service auditor should take appropriate action, which may include the following:

- Obtaining legal advice about the consequences of different courses of action
- Communicating with those charged with governance of the service organization
- Disclaiming an opinion, modifying the service auditor's opinion, or adding an emphasis paragraph
- Communicating with third parties (for example, a regulator) when required to do so
- Withdrawing from the engagement

3.86 If, as a result of performing the examination procedures, the service auditor becomes aware that any identified deviations have resulted from intentional acts by service organization personnel, the service auditor reassesses the risk that management's description of the service organization's system is not fairly presented; the controls are not suitably designed; the controls are not operating effectively; and if the report addresses the privacy principle, the service organization has not complied with the commitments in its statement of privacy practices. Additionally, depending on the nature of any intentional acts that are identified and the level of responsibility of the service organization personnel involved in those acts (for example, senior management versus clerical personnel), the service auditor considers the effect of the intentional act on the engagement and whether it is appropriate for the service auditor to continue with, or withdraw from, the engagement.

3.87 If the service auditor becomes aware of incidents of noncompliance with laws and regulations or other adverse events that have not been prevented or detected by a control and that may affect one or more user entities, the service auditor should determine the effect of such incidents on management's description of the service organization's system; the suitability of the design and operating effectiveness of the controls; if the report addresses the privacy principle, the service organization's compliance with the commitments in its statement of privacy practices; and the service auditor's report.

3.88 Paragraph 4.33 of this guide presents an illustrative explanatory paragraph that would be added to the service auditor's report when controls are not operating effectively.

Obtaining Written Representation

3.89 As indicated in paragraph 2.01 of this guide, one of the conditions for accepting or continuing an engagement to report on controls at a service organization is that management of the service organization agrees to the terms of the engagement by acknowledging and accepting its responsibility for providing the service auditor with written representations at the conclusion of the engagement.

3.90 The service auditor should request management to provide written representations that

     a. reaffirm its assertion that is attached to the description of the service organization's system.

     b. it has provided the service auditor with all relevant information and access agreed to.

     c. it has disclosed to the service auditor any of the following of which it is aware:

         i. Instances of noncompliance with laws and regulations or uncorrected errors attributable to the service organization that may affect one or more user entities.

         ii. Knowledge of (1) any actual, suspected, or alleged intentional acts by management or the service organization's employees that could adversely affect the fairness of the presentation of management's description of the service organization's system or (2) whether the controls stated in the description were suitably designed and operating effectively to meet the applicable trust services criteria.

         iii. Design deficiencies in controls.

         iv. Instances when controls have not operated as described.

         v. Any instances of noncompliance regarding its commitments set forth in its statement of privacy practices.

         vi. Any events subsequent to the period covered by management's description of the service organization's system up to the date of the service auditor's report that could have a significant effect on management's assertion or the fact that no such subsequent events have occurred.

3.91 If a service organization uses a subservice organization, and management's description of the service organization's system uses the inclusive method, the service auditor also should obtain written representations from management of the subservice organization that address the matters identified in paragraph 3.90.

3.92 The service auditor may consider it necessary to request written representations about matters in addition to those listed in paragraph 3.90, including oral representations for which no other evidential matter exists. This would be determined based on the facts and circumstances of the particular engagement (for example, if changes to the service organization's controls have occurred during the period covered by the service auditor's report, there might be a need to obtain representations that address the periods before and after the change).

3.93 The written representations required by paragraph 3.90 are separate from, and in addition to, management's written assertion.

3.94 The written representations should be in the form of a representation letter addressed to the service auditor, signed by the individuals identified by the service auditor, and dated as of the same date as the service auditor's report.

3.95 If management does not provide one or more of the requested representations, the service auditor should do the following:

- Discuss the matter with management
- Evaluate the effect of such refusal on the service auditor's assessment of the integrity of management and evaluate the effect that this may have on the reliability of management's representations and evidence in general
- Take appropriate actions, which may include disclaiming an opinion or withdrawing from the engagement

3.96 If management refuses to provide the service auditor with (a) representations that reaffirm its assertion or (b) a representation that it has provided the service auditor with all relevant information and access agreed to, the service auditor should disclaim an opinion or withdraw from the engagement. This is the case because these representations are fundamental to the engagement and affect all the other representations made by management and other service organization personnel during the course of the engagement.

3.97 If the service auditor is unable to obtain written representations regarding relevant trust services criteria and related controls at the subservice organization, management of the service organization would be unable to use the inclusive method but may be able to use the carve-out method.

3.98 Because management's written representations are an important consideration when forming the service auditor's opinion, the service auditor ordinarily would not be able to issue his or her report until he or she received the representation letter. Illustrative representation letters for a service auditor's engagement are presented in appendix C, "Illustrative Management Assertions and Related Service Auditor's Reports on Controls at a Service Organization Relevant to Security, Availability, Processing Integrity, Confidentiality, or Privacy," of this guide.

Subsequent Events

3.99 The service auditor makes inquiries about whether management is aware of any events subsequent to the period covered by management's description of the service organization's system up to the date of the service auditor's report that could have a significant effect on management's assertion and the underlying subject matter of the assertion. If the service auditor becomes aware, through inquiry or otherwise, of such an event or any other event that is of such a nature and significance that its disclosure is necessary to prevent users of the report from being misled, and information about that event is not disclosed by management in its description, the service auditor should modify his or her opinion on the fairness of the presentation of the description and disclose the event in the service auditor's report. The service auditor is responsible for determining the effect of the event on the service auditor's report, regardless of whether management appropriately discloses the event and modifies its written assertion.

3.100   The following are examples of subsequent events that could affect management's assertion or description of the service organization's system:

- After the period covered by the service auditor's report, management discovered that during the last quarter of the period covered by the service auditor's report, the IT security director provided all the programmers with access to the production data files, enabling them to modify data.

- After the period covered by the service auditor's report, management discovered that a confidentiality breach occurred at the service organization during the period covered by the service auditor's report.

- After the period covered by the service auditor's report, it was discovered that during the examination period, the signatures on a number of nonautomated transaction execution instructions that appeared to be authenticated by signature verification were not authenticated.

3.101   There may be situations in which the event discovered subsequent to the period covered by management's description of the service organization's system up to the date of the service auditor's report would likely have no effect on management's assertion because the underlying situation did not occur or exist until after the period covered by management's description of the service organization's system; however, the matter may be sufficiently important for disclosure by management in its description and, potentially, the service auditor in an emphasis paragraph of the service auditor's report. The following are examples of such subsequent events:

- The service organization was acquired by another entity.

- The service organization experienced a significant operating disruption.

- A data center-hosting service organization that provides applications and technology that enable user entities to perform essential business functions made significant changes to its information systems, including a system conversion or significant outsourcing of operations.

The service organization may wish to disclose such events in a separate section of the description of the service organization's system titled, for example, "Other Information Provided by the Service Organization."

3.102 The service auditor has no responsibility to keep informed of events subsequent to the date of the service auditor's report; however, after the release of the service auditor's report, the service auditor may become aware of conditions that existed at the report date that might have affected management's assertion and the service auditor's report had the service auditor been aware of them. The evaluation of such subsequent information is similar to the evaluation of information discovered subsequent to the date of the report on an audit of financial statements, as described in AU section 561, *Subsequent Discovery of Facts Existing at the Date of the Auditor's Report* (AICPA, *Professional Standards*). The service auditor should adapt and apply the guidance in AU section 561.

Documentation

3.103 Paragraphs .100–.107 of AT section 101 describe the service auditor's responsibilities related to documentation. In addition, the service auditor considers whether users in certain industry segments (for example, government) may require additional documentation.

Consideration of Management's Assertion

3.104 Management may have provided the service auditor with an assertion at the beginning of the engagement that includes all the relevant aspects that would be expected. The service auditor may identify deficiencies in the operating effectiveness of controls that cause the service auditor to qualify the opinion. In this instance, the service auditor would evaluate the reason why management had not identified the deficiencies in the operating effectiveness of the controls and determine whether management should have known these existed and whether management is in a position to be able to provide the assertion or whether additional work needs to be done by management before they provide the final assertion that is attached to the description. In instances in which the service auditor has identified deficiencies that give rise to a qualification in the opinion, management is expected to modify their assertion to note those deficiencies.

3.105 The service auditor may determine that management's assertion does not provide sufficient detail, fails to disclose deficiencies identified by the service auditor that resulted in a qualified opinion, or contains inaccuracies. In these situations, the service auditor should request that management modify its assertion. For example, when deviations identified in the examination cause the service auditor to qualify the opinion, the service auditor should ask management to amend its assertion to reflect the identified deficiencies. If management refuses to do so, the service auditor takes appropriate action, which may include additional modifications to the service auditor's report, rendering an adverse opinion, or withdrawing from the engagement.

Chapter 4

Reporting

This chapter describes the service auditor's responsibilities when reporting on a service organization's controls relevant to security, availability, processing integrity, confidentiality, or privacy. This chapter primarily focuses on the elements of a service auditor's report and modifications to the service auditor's opinion.

Responsibilities of the Service Auditor

4.01 The service auditor's responsibilities for reporting on a service organization controls (SOC) 2 engagement include the following:

- Preparing the service auditor's report, including all the report elements identified in paragraph 4.02, and modifying the report if the service auditor determines it is appropriate to do so
- For a type 2 report, preparing a written description of the tests of controls performed by the service auditor and the results of those tests
- For a type 2 report that addresses the privacy principle, preparing a written description of the service auditor's tests of the service organization's compliance with the commitments in its statement of privacy practices and the results of those tests

Contents of the Service Auditor's Report

4.02 A service auditor's type 2 report on controls relevant to security, availability, processing integrity, confidentiality, or privacy should include the following elements:

    a. A title that includes the word *independent.*

    b. An addressee.

    c. Identification of the following:

        i. Management's description of the service organization's system and the function performed by the system or service provided by the service organization.

        ii. Any parts of management's description of the service organization's system that are not covered by the service auditor's report.

        iii. The criteria for evaluating whether management's description of the service organization's system is fairly presented.

        iv. The applicable trust services criteria for evaluating whether controls are suitably designed and operating effectively.

        v. When the report addresses the privacy principle, the service organization's statement of privacy practices.

      vi. Any services performed by a subservice organization and whether the carve-out method or inclusive method was used in relation to them. Depending on which method is used, the following should be included:

        (1) If the carve-out method was used, a statement that management's description of the service organization's system excludes controls of the subservice organization, and when the report addresses the privacy principle, that the description also excludes the subservice organization's statement of privacy practices and that the service auditor's procedures do not extend to the subservice organization.

        (2) If the inclusive method was used, a statement that management's description of the service organization's system includes applicable trust services criteria and controls for the subservice organization, and when the report addresses the privacy principle, that the description also includes the subservice organization's statement of privacy practices and that the service auditor's procedures included procedures related to the subservice organization.

    d. If management's description of the service organization's system refers to the need for complementary user-entity controls, a statement that the service auditor has not evaluated the suitability of the design or operating effectiveness of complementary user-entity controls and that the applicable trust services criteria stated in the description can be met only if complementary user-entity controls are suitably designed and operating effectively, along with the related controls at the service organization.

    e. A reference to management's assertion and a statement that management is responsible for the following:

      i. Preparing the description of the service organization's system; the assertion; and when the report covers controls over privacy, the statement of privacy practices, including the completeness, accuracy, and method of presentation of the description, assertion, and statement of privacy practices.

      ii. Providing the services covered by the description of the service organization's system.

      iii. Selecting the trust services principle(s) being reported on and stating the applicable trust services criteria and related controls in the description of the service organization's system.

      iv. Identifying any applicable trust services criteria relevant to the principle being reported on that have been omitted from the description and explaining the reason for the omission.

     v. Designing, implementing, and documenting controls that are suitably designed and operating effectively to meet the applicable trust services criteria.

    vi. When the report covers controls over privacy, complying with the commitments in its statement of privacy practices included in, or attached to, the description of the service organization's system.

f. A statement that the service auditor's responsibility is to express an opinion on the fairness of the presentation of management's description of the service organization's system; the suitability of the design and operating effectiveness of the controls to meet the applicable trust services criteria; and when the report addresses the privacy principle, the service organization's compliance with the commitments in its statement of privacy practices, based on the service auditor's examination.

g. A statement that the examination was conducted in accordance with attestation standards established by the American Institute of Certified Public Accountants and that those standards require the service auditor to plan and perform the examination to obtain reasonable assurance about whether management's description of the service organization's system is fairly presented; whether the controls are suitably designed and operating effectively throughout the specified period to meet the applicable trust services criteria; and if the report addresses the privacy principle, whether the service organization complied with the commitments in its statement of privacy practices.

h. A statement that an examination of management's description of a service organization's system and the suitability of the design and operating effectiveness of controls involves performing procedures to obtain evidence about the following:

    i. The fairness of the presentation of the description.

    ii. The suitability of the design and operating effectiveness of the controls to meet the applicable trust services criteria.

    iii. If the report addresses the privacy principle, the service organization's compliance with the commitments in its statement of privacy practices.

i. A statement that the examination included assessing the risks that management's description of the service organization's system is not fairly presented; that the controls were not suitably designed or operating effectively to meet the applicable trust services criteria; and if the report addresses the privacy principle, that the service organization did not comply with the commitments in its statement of privacy practices.

j. A statement that the examination also included testing the operating effectiveness of those controls that the service auditor considers necessary to provide reasonable assurance that the applicable trust services criteria were met, and if the report addresses the privacy principle, testing the service organization's compliance with the commitments in its statement of privacy practices.

k. A statement that the service auditor believes the examination provides a reasonable basis for his or her opinion.

l. A statement about the inherent limitations of controls, including the risk of projecting to future periods any evaluation of the fairness of the presentation of management's description of the service organization's system or conclusions about the suitability of the design or operating effectiveness of controls, and when the report addresses the privacy principle, the service organization's compliance with the commitments in its statement of privacy practices.

m. The service auditor's opinion on whether, in all material respects, based on the criteria described in management's assertion

    i. management's description of the service organization's system fairly presents the service organization's system that was designed and implemented throughout the specified period.

    ii. the controls related to the applicable trust services criteria were suitably designed to provide reasonable assurance that those criteria would be met if the controls operated effectively throughout the specified period.

    iii. the controls that the service auditor tested, which were those necessary to provide reasonable assurance that the applicable trust services criteria were met, operated effectively throughout the specified period.

    iv. if the report addresses the privacy principle, the service organization complied with the commitments in its statement of privacy practices throughout the specified period.

n. If the application of complementary user-entity controls is necessary to meet the applicable trust services criteria, a reference to this condition.

o. A reference to a part of the service auditor's report that contains a description of the service auditor's tests of controls and the results thereof and that includes the following:

    i. Identification of each of the applicable trust services criteria, the controls that were tested, whether the items tested for each control represent all or a selection of the items in the population, and the nature of the tests in sufficient detail to enable users of the report to determine the effect of such tests on their risk assessments.

    ii. If deviations have been identified in the operation of controls included in the description, the extent of testing performed by the service auditor that led to the identification of the deviations, including the number of items tested, and the number and nature of the deviations noted, even if, on the basis of tests performed, the service auditor concludes that the related criteria were met.

p. If the report addresses the privacy principle, a reference to a part of the service auditor's report that contains a description of the service auditor's tests of compliance with the service organization's commitments in its statement of privacy practices and the results thereof and that includes the following:

    i. Identification of the commitments that were tested, whether the items tested for each commitment represent all or a selection of the items in the population, and the nature of the tests in sufficient detail to enable users of the report to determine the effect of such tests on their risk assessments.

ii. If deviations have been identified in the service organization's compliance with the commitments in its statement of privacy practices, the extent of testing performed by the service auditor that led to the identification of the deviations, including the number of items tested, and the number and nature of the deviations noted, even if, on the basis of tests performed, the service auditor concludes that the related commitment was complied with.

q. A statement indicating that the service auditor's report is intended solely for the information and use of management of the service organization and other specified parties.

r. The date of the service auditor's report.

s. The name of the service auditor and the city and state where the service auditor maintains the office that has responsibility for the engagement.

Describing Tests and the Results of Tests in a Type 2 Report [1]

4.03   A service auditor's type 2 report should contain a reference to a description of the service auditor's tests of controls and the results of those tests. If the type 2 report addresses the privacy principle, it should also contain a reference to a description of the service auditor's tests of the service organization's compliance with the commitments in its statement of privacy practices. The description should identify the controls and any privacy commitments that were tested, whether the items tested represent all or a selection of the items in the population, and the nature of the tests performed in sufficient detail to enable users to determine the effect of such tests on the user's particular objectives.

4.04   The concept of materiality is not applicable when reporting the results of tests for which deviations have been identified because the service auditor does not have the ability to determine whether a deviation will be relevant to a particular user. Consequently, the service auditor reports all deviations. If the service auditor has not identified any deviations, the service auditor may document those results with a phrase such as "No deviations noted."

4.05   The description of tests need not be a duplication of the service auditor's detailed work program, which might make the report too voluminous for users and provide more than the required level of detail. The service auditor is not required to indicate the size of the sample, unless deviations were identified during testing.

4.06   If deviations have been identified, the service auditor's description of tests and results should identify the extent of testing performed by the service

---

[1] For brevity, the word *tests* as used hereinafter refers to tests of the operating effectiveness of controls or tests of the service organization's compliance with the commitments in its statement of privacy practices, unless otherwise specified.

auditor that led to the identification of the deviations, including the number of items tested and the number and nature of the deviations noted, even if, on the basis of tests performed, the service auditor concludes that the applicable trust services criteria were met, and the service organization complied with the commitments in its statement of privacy practices.

4.07 If deviations are identified, it may be helpful to users of the report for management to disclose, to the extent known, the causative factors for the deviation, the controls that mitigate the effect of the deviation, corrective actions taken, and other qualitative factors that would assist users in understanding the effect of the deviations. Such information may be included in an attachment to the description titled "Other Information Provided by Example Service Organization That Is Not Covered by the Service Auditor's Report" or in the description and referred to in the service auditor's tests and results. If such information is included in the description, the service auditor would need to corroborate such information through inquiry, inspection of documentation, and other procedures. Information provided by management about controls that mitigate the effect of deviations or corrective actions should not include forward-looking information, such as future plans to implement controls.

4.08 The following example illustrates the documentation of tests of controls for which deviations have been identified. It is assumed that in each situation, other relevant controls and tests of controls would also be described:

- *Criteria.* Procedures exist to restrict physical access to the defined system, including, but not limited to, facilities; backup media; and other system components, such as firewalls, routers, and servers.

- *Example Service Organization's controls.* Security personnel deactivate physical security access cards of terminated employees on a daily basis using a list generated by the human resources system.

- *Service auditor's tests of controls.* Selected a sample of terminated employees from a list generated by the human resources system and compared the termination date with the access card deactivation date for each employee.

- *Results of tests of controls.* For one terminated employee in an initial sample of 25, the employee's physical access security card was not deactivated until 90 days after the employee's last day of work. In an additional sample of 15 terminated employees, no additional deviations were noted.

- *Management's response.* The terminated employee's name was not listed on the report from the human resources system until 90 days after termination. Subsequent investigation determined that the report used for removing physical access was generated based on the last payroll date of the employee, rather than the last date employed. This employee was 1 of 15 employees who were a part of a reduction in force and received the severance benefit. These employees each continued on the payroll system for 90 days after termination. The physical access cards of all employees receiving severance have been deactivated, and in addition, the report from the human resources system has been changed to generate the list based on the last date of employment.

Describing Tests and Results When Using the Internal Audit Function

4.09 If the work of the internal audit function has been used, the service auditor should not make reference to that work in the service auditor's opinion. Notwithstanding its degree of autonomy and objectivity, the internal audit function is not independent of the service organization. The service auditor has sole responsibility for the opinion expressed in the service auditor's report, and accordingly, that responsibility is not reduced by the service auditor's use of the work of the internal audit function.

4.10 If the work of the internal audit function has been used in performing tests of controls, the part of the service auditor's report that describes the service auditor's tests of controls and the results thereof should include a description of the internal auditor's work and the service auditor's procedures with respect to that work. The phrase "using the work of the internal audit function" is derived from AU section 322, *The Auditor's Consideration of the Internal Audit Function in an Audit of Financial Statements* (AICPA, *Professional Standards*), and refers to work designed and performed by the internal audit function on its own. This would include tests of controls designed and performed by the internal audit function during the period covered by the type 2 report. If the service auditor uses members of the service organization's internal audit function to provide direct assistance, including assistance in performing tests of controls that are designed by the service auditor and performed under the direction, supervision, and review of the service auditor, the description of tests of controls and results need not distinguish between the tests performed by members of the internal audit function and the tests performed by the service auditor because when the internal audit function provides direct assistance, the work performed by the internal audit function undergoes the same scrutiny as if it were performed by the service auditor's staff. When the service auditor uses members of the service organization's internal audit function to provide direct assistance, the service auditor should adapt and apply the requirements in paragraph .27 of AU section 322.

4.11 The service auditor's description of tests of controls performed by the internal audit function and the service auditor's procedures with respect to that work may be presented in a number of ways (for example, by including introductory material in the description of tests of controls indicating that certain work of the internal audit function was used in performing tests of controls or by specifically identifying the tests performed by the internal audit function and attributing those tests to the internal audit function).

4.12 The following are examples of introductory material that may be included in the description of tests of controls and results to inform readers that the service auditor has used the work of the internal audit function to perform tests of controls:

- Throughout the examination period, members of XYZ Service Organization's internal audit function performed tests of controls related to the following criterion: procedures exist to restrict logical access to the defined system, including distribution of output restricted to authorized users. Members of the internal audit function observed the controls being performed by employees, inspected documentation of the performance of the control, and reperformed a sample of control activities. The tests performed by the members of the internal audit function and the results of those tests are presented under the captions "Tests Performed" and "Results of Tests." We reperformed selected tests that had been performed by members of the internal audit function and found no exceptions.

- Members of XYZ Service Organization's internal audit function performed tests of controls for the following criterion: procedures exist to restrict logical access to the defined system, including distribution of output restricted to authorized users. The tests performed by members of the internal audit function included inquiry of employees who performed the control activities, observation of the control being performed at different times during the examination period, reperformance, and examination of the documentation for a sample of requests for system access and a sample of requests for reports. The tests performed by the members of the internal audit function and the results of those tests are presented under the captions "Tests Performed" and "Results of Tests." We tested the work of members of the internal audit function through a combination of independent testing and reperformance and noted no exceptions.

Modifications of the Service Auditor's Report

4.13   The service auditor's opinion should be modified, and the service auditor's report should contain a clear description of all the reasons for the modification if the service auditor concludes that

- *a.* management's description of the service organization's system is not fairly presented, in all material respects;

- *b.* the controls are not suitably designed to provide reasonable assurance that the applicable trust services criteria would be met if the controls operated as described;

- *c.* in the case of a type 2 report, the controls did not operate effectively throughout the specified period to meet the applicable trust services criteria stated in management's description of the service organization's system;

- *d.* a scope limitation exists, resulting in the service auditor's inability to obtain sufficient appropriate evidence; or

- *e.* in the case of a type 2 report that addresses the privacy principle, the service organization did not comply with the commitments in its statement of privacy practices.

4.14   When determining whether to modify the service auditor's report, the service auditor considers the individual and aggregate effect of identified deviations in management's description of the service organization's system and the suitability of the design and operating effectiveness of the controls throughout the specified period. The service auditor considers quantitative and qualitative factors, such as the following:

- The nature and cause of the deviations

- The tolerable rate of deviations that the service auditor has established

- The pervasiveness of the deviations (for example, whether more than one criterion would be affected)
- The likelihood that the deviations are indicators of control deficiencies that will result in failure to meet the applicable trust services criteria
- The magnitude of such failures that could occur as a result of control deficiencies
- Whether users could be misled if the service auditor's opinion or individual components of the opinion were not modified

4.15 If the service auditor decides that his or her opinion should be modified, the report should contain a clear description of all the reasons for the modification. The objective of that description is to enable report users to develop their own assessments of the effect of deficiencies and deviations on users.

4.16 If a modified opinion is appropriate, the service auditor determines whether to issue a qualified opinion, an adverse opinion, or a disclaimer of opinion.

4.17 When the service auditor has determined that a qualified opinion is appropriate, in addition to adding an explanatory paragraph to the service auditor's report before the opinion paragraph, the service auditor should also modify the opinion paragraph of the service auditor's report as follows (new language is shown in boldface italics; deleted language is shown in strikethrough):

> In our opinion, ~~in all material respects~~ *except for the matter referred to in the preceding paragraph,* based on the description criteria identified in [*name of service organization*]'s assertion and the applicable trust services criteria, *in all material respects* . . .

4.18 When the service auditor has determined that an adverse opinion is appropriate, in addition to adding an explanatory paragraph to the report that precedes the opinion paragraph and explains all the substantive reasons for the adverse opinion and the principal effects on the subject matter of the report, the service auditor should also modify the opinion paragraph of the service auditor's report. The following is an example of such a paragraph when the service auditor is expressing an adverse opinion on all three components of the opinion (new language is shown in boldface italics; deleted language is shown in strikethrough):

> In our opinion, ~~in all material respects~~ *because of the matter referred to in the preceding paragraph,* based on the description criteria identified in [*name of service organization*]'s assertion and the applicable trust services criteria
>
> a. the description *does not* ~~fairly~~ presents the [*type or name of system*] that was designed and implemented throughout the period [*date*] to [*date*].
>
> b. the controls stated in the description were *not* suitably designed to provide reasonable assurance that the applicable trust services criteria would be met if the controls operated effectively throughout the period [*date*] to [*date*].
>
> c. the controls tested, which were those necessary to provide reasonable assurance that the criteria stated in the description were met, *did not* operate~~d~~ effectively throughout the period [*date*] to [*date*].

4.19 In some circumstances, the service auditor may decide to disclaim an opinion because he or she is unable to obtain sufficient appropriate evidence but, based on the limited procedures performed, has concluded that certain aspects of management's description of the service organization's system are not fairly presented, certain controls are not suitably designed, or certain controls did not operate effectively. In these circumstances, the service auditor should identify these findings in his or her report. The service auditor may also disclaim an opinion if management of the service organization fails to provide both a written assertion or an appropriate letter of representations.

4.20 If the service auditor disclaims an opinion, the service auditor's report should not identify the procedures that were performed nor include statements describing the characteristics of a service auditor's engagement because to do so might overshadow the disclaimer. When disclaiming an opinion, in addition to adding an explanatory paragraph to the service auditor's report that describes the reason for the disclaimer and any deficiencies identified by the service auditor, the opinion paragraph would be replaced by the following disclaimer of opinion: (new language is shown in boldface italics):

> *Because of the matter described in the preceding paragraph, the scope of our work was not sufficient to enable us to express, and we do not express, an opinion.*

Illustrative Explanatory Paragraphs When the Description Is Not Fairly Presented

4.21 A number of situations are presented in chapter 3, "Performing the Engagement," of this guide in which the service auditor determines that the description is not fairly presented. In practice, if the service auditor makes such a determination, the service auditor would discuss the matter with management of the service organization, describe the changes that need to be made for the description to be fairly presented, and ask management to amend the description to include the omitted information or correct the misstated information. The following paragraphs contain examples of explanatory paragraphs that would be inserted before the modified opinion paragraph of the service auditor's report if management is unwilling to amend a description that is not fairly presented. For all these paragraphs, the service auditor would modify the opinion paragraph as follows (new language is shown in boldface italics; deleted language is shown in strikethrough):

> In our opinion, ~~in all material respects~~ *except for the matter referred to in the preceding paragraph,* based on the description criteria identified in [*name of service organization*]'s assertion and the applicable trust services criteria, *in all material respects* . . .

4.22 The following is an example of an explanatory paragraph that would be added to the service auditor's report when the description includes controls that have not been implemented:

> The accompanying description states that Example Service Organization's system is protected against unauthorized logical access through the use of operator identification numbers and passwords. Based on inquiries of staff personnel and observation of activities, we determined that operator identification numbers and passwords are used in applications A and B but are not used in application C.

4.23 The following is an example of an explanatory paragraph that would be added to the service auditor's report when the functions and processing performed by a subservice organization are significant to the users, and the service organization has not disclosed that it uses a subservice organization and the functions that the subservice organization performs:

> Example Trust Organization's description does not indicate that it uses a subservice organization for information processing, which we believe could be significant to users because controls at the subservice organization over changes to programs, as well as physical and logical access to system resources, would be relevant to users.

4.24 If management of the service organization inappropriately omits one or more applicable trust services criteria from the description of the service organization's system, the service auditor should request that management include the omitted criteria and related controls. If management refuses to do so, the service auditor should disclaim an opinion or withdraw from the engagement.

Identifying Information That Is Not Covered by the Service Auditor's Report

4.25 The service organization may wish to attach to the description of the service organization's system, or include in a document containing the service auditor's report, information in addition to its description. The following are examples of such information:

- Future plans for new systems
- Other services provided by the service organization that are not included in the scope of the engagement
- Qualitative information, such as marketing claims, that may not be objectively measurable
- Responses from management to deviations identified by the service auditor when such responses have not been subject to procedures by the service auditor

4.26 Paragraph 3.16 of this guide states that such other information should be distinguished from the service organization's description of its system by excluding the information from the description. It also states that if the other information is attached to the description or included in a document that contains the description of the service organization's system and the service auditor's report, the other information should be differentiated from the information covered by the service auditor's report, for example, through the use of a title such as "Other Information Provided by Example Service Organization That Is Not Covered by the Service Auditor's Report."

4.27 Because of the nature of the other information or its presentation, the service auditor may wish to add an explanatory paragraph to the service auditor's report indicating that the other information is not covered by the service auditor's report. The following is an example of such a paragraph:

> The information attached to the description titled "Other Information Provided by Example Service Organization That Is Not Covered by the Service Auditor's Report" describes the service organization's medical billing system. It is presented by the management of Example Service

Organization to provide additional information and is not a part of the service organization's description of its medical records management system made available to user entities during the period from June 1, 20X0, to May 31, 20X1. Information about Example Service Organization's medical billing system has not been subjected to the procedures applied in the examination of the description of the medical records management system and the suitability of the design and operating effectiveness of controls to meet the related criteria stated in the description of the medical records management system.

4.28   The service auditor also has the option of disclaiming an opinion on information that is not covered by the service auditor's report by adding the words "and accordingly, we express no opinion on it" at the end of the explanatory paragraph illustrated in paragraph 4.27.

Illustrative Explanatory Paragraphs: Controls Are Not Suitably Designed

4.29   The following is an example of an explanatory paragraph that would be added to the service auditor's report, preceding the opinion paragraph, if the service auditor concludes that controls are not suitably designed to meet an applicable trust services criterion:

> The accompanying description of ABC Service Organization's system states on page 8 that ABC Service Organization's system supervisor makes changes to the systems only if the changes are authorized, tested, and documented. The procedures, however, do not include a requirement for approval of the change before the change is placed into operation. As a result, the controls are not suitably designed to meet the following criterion: controls provide reasonable assurance that only authorized, tested, and documented changes are made to the system.

4.30   The service auditor may conclude that the controls are not suitably designed to meet part of a criterion. The following is an example of an explanatory paragraph that would be added to the service auditor's report, preceding the opinion paragraph, if the service auditor determines that controls are not suitably designed to meet part of a criterion:

> The criteria for the privacy principle includes the following criterion: personal information is provided to the individual in an understandable form; in a reasonable time frame; and at a reasonable cost, if any. Attempts to access the system using an authenticated identity indicated that the design of the control requires users with authenticated identities to wait 24 hours before being granted access to their personal information. As a result, the authentication control is not suitably designed to meet the aforementioned criteria.

4.31   The service auditor focuses on the suitability of the design of controls to meet the related applicable trust services criteria during the period covered by the service auditor's report, not the suitability of the design of controls to meet criteria in future periods when conditions may change. For example, if computer programs are correctly processing data during the period covered by the service auditor's report, and the design of the controls will need to be changed in future periods to accommodate conditions that will exist in the future, the service auditor would not be required to report this information as a design deficiency in his or her report.[2] However, if a service auditor becomes aware of the need for change to the design of controls at the service organization to address future conditions, the service auditor, in his or her judgment, may choose to communicate this information to the service organization's management and may consider advising management to disclose this information and its plans for changing the design of its controls to address the expected future conditions in a section of the service auditor's document titled "Other Information Provided by the Service Organization That Is Not Covered by the Service Auditor's Report."

Controls Were Not Suitably Designed During a Portion of the Period

4.32 The following is an example of an explanatory paragraph that would be added to the service auditor's report, preceding the opinion paragraph, if the service auditor concludes that controls are not suitably designed to meet an applicable trust services criterion for a portion of the period under examination until an additional control was added:

> The accompanying description of ABC Service Organization's system states on page 8 that ABC Service Organization's system supervisor makes changes to the systems only if the changes are authorized, tested, and documented. The procedures, however, did not include a requirement for approval of the change before the change is placed into operation during the period [date] to [date]. On [date], ABC Service Organization implemented a procedure requiring all changes to be reviewed and approved by the director of application development prior to the change to the system. As a result, the controls were not suitably designed to meet the following criterion during the period [date] to [date]: controls provide reasonable assurance that only authorized, tested, and documented changes are made to the system.

Illustrative Explanatory Paragraph: Controls Are Not Operating Effectively

4.33 The service auditor may conclude that controls are suitably designed but are not operating effectively to meet one or more of the applicable trust services criteria. The following is an example of an explanatory paragraph that may be added to the service auditor's report, preceding the opinion paragraph, if the service auditor determines that controls are not operating effectively:

> ABC Service Organization states in the description of its system that the director of IT may approve emergency changes to the system without receiving a written request for such changes, as long as the changes are documented within 48 hours after implementation into production. However, as noted on page 155 of the description of tests of controls and the results thereof, controls related to the authorization of emergency changes were not performed and, therefore, were not operating effectively throughout the period [date] to [date]. This control deficiency

---

[2] See paragraph A39 of Statement on Standards for Attestation Engagements No. 16, *Reporting on Controls at a Service Organization* (AICPA, *Professional Standards*, AT sec. 801), for similar guidance related to internal control over financial reporting.

resulted in not meeting the following criterion: procedures exist to provide that emergency changes are documented and authorized in a timely manner.

In addition, the service auditor modifies the opinion paragraph of the service auditor's report on operating effectiveness as follows (new language is shown in boldface italics; deleted language is shown in strikethrough):

In our opinion, ~~in all material respects,~~ *except for the matter described in the preceding paragraph,* based on the description criteria identified in [*name of service organization*]'s assertion and the applicable trust services criteria, *in all material respects* . . .

Scope Limitation: Service Auditor Is Unable to Obtain Sufficient Appropriate Evidence

4.34 The following is an example of an explanatory paragraph that would be added to the service auditor's report if the service auditor is unable to obtain sufficient appropriate evidence regarding the operating effectiveness of controls to meet a criterion:

The accompanying description of ABC Service Organization's system states on page 45 that ABC Service Organization makes system changes only if they are authorized, tested, and documented. Documentation of the authorization and testing of proposed system changes was destroyed on July 15, 20X0, and we were unable to obtain sufficient evidence that system changes were authorized and tested prior to July 15, 20X0. As a result, we were unable to determine whether controls were operating effectively during the period January 1, 20X0, to July 14, 20X0, to meet the following criterion: procedures exist to provide that only authorized, tested, and documented changes are made to the system.

Reporting on Compliance With the Commitments in the Statement of Privacy Practices When the Type 2 Report Addresses the Privacy Principle

4.35 A service auditor's type 2 report that covers controls over privacy includes the service auditor's opinion on whether the service organization complied with the commitments in its statement of privacy practices throughout the period covered by the service auditor's report. The following are situations that may result in a modification of the service auditor's report:

- The statement of privacy practices is not included with management's description of the service organization's system or is incomplete.
- Privacy commitments are not clearly described in management's privacy statement.
- The results of tests performed do not provide sufficient appropriate evidence to conclude that the service organization complied with the commitments in its statement of privacy practices throughout the examination period.

4.36 The following are examples of explanatory paragraphs that may be added to the service auditor's report, preceding the opinion paragraph, if the service auditor determines that the service organization did not comply with the commitments in its statement of privacy practices (new language is shown in boldface italics; deleted language is shown in strikethrough):

- The accompanying statement of privacy practices states on page 40 that Example Service Organization requires all vendors with whom it shares personal information to sign a data-sharing agreement requiring these vendors to adhere to privacy practices similar to those established by Example Service Organization. The results of our tests indicated that two vendors with whom personal information was shared had not signed a data-sharing agreement. As a result, the following commitment was not met: all vendors with whom the service organization shares personal information are required to sign a data-sharing agreement that requires these vendors to follow privacy practices similar to ours.

  In our opinion, ~~in all material respects,~~ *except for the matter described in the preceding paragraph,* based on the description criteria identified in [*name of service organization*]'s assertion and the applicable trust services criteria, *in all material respects . . .*

- Example Service Organization states in its statement of privacy practices on page [*aa*] that Example Service Organization securely disposes of all copies, including archived and backup copies, of personal information records. However, as noted on page 45 of the description of tests of controls and the results thereof, backup copies of records were not disposed of securely. This results in a failure to meet the following commitment of the service organization: archived and backup copies of personal information are disposed of securely.

  In our opinion, ~~in all material respects,~~ *except for the matter described in the preceding paragraph,* based on the description criteria identified in [*name of service organization*]'s assertion and the applicable trust services criteria, *in all material respects . . .*

Reporting When the Service Organization Uses the Carve-Out Method to Present a Subservice Organization

4.37 The following are modifications to the scope paragraph of a type 2 report for use in engagements in which the service organization uses a subservice organization and presents its description using the carve-out method (new language is shown in boldface italics):

Scope

We have examined the attached description titled "XYZ Service Organization's Description of the Adaptable Cloud Computing System for the Period January 1, 200X, to December 31, 200X"[3] (the description) and the suitability of the design and operating effectiveness of controls to meet the criteria for the privacy principle set forth in TSP section

---

[3] The title of the description of the service organization's system in the service auditor's report should match the title used by management of the service organization in its description.

100, *Trust Services Principles, Criteria, and Illustrations for Security, Availability, Processing Integrity, Confidentiality, and Privacy* (AICPA, *Technical Practice Aids*) (applicable trust services criteria), throughout the period January 1, 20X1, to December 31, 20X1.

XYZ Service Organization uses a service organization (subservice organization) to perform certain processing of customers' personal information. The description indicates that certain applicable trust services criteria can only be met if controls at the subservice organization are suitably designed and operating effectively. The description presents XYZ Service Organization's system; its controls relevant to the applicable trust services criteria; and the types of controls that the service organization expects to be implemented, suitably designed, and operating effectively at the subservice organization to meet certain applicable trust services criteria. The description does not include any of the controls implemented at the subservice organization. Our examination did not extend to the services provided by the subservice organization or the subservice organization's compliance with the commitments in its statement of privacy practices.

4.38 Following are modifications to the applicable subparagraphs of the opinion paragraph of a type 2 report for use in engagements in which the service organization uses a subservice organization and presents its description using the carve-out method (new language is shown in boldface italics):

In our opinion, in all material respects, based on the description criteria identified in XYZ Service Organization's assertion and the applicable trust services criteria

a. the description fairly presents XYZ Service Organization's [*type or name of*] system and the related privacy practices that were designed and implemented throughout the period [*date*] to [*date*].

b. the controls stated in the description were suitably designed to provide reasonable assurance that the applicable trust services criteria would be met if the controls operated effectively throughout the period [*date*] to [*date*], ***and the subservice organization applied, throughout the period [date] to [date], the types of controls expected to be implemented at the subservice organization and incorporated in the design of the system***.

c. the controls we tested, which ***together with the types of controls expected to be implemented at the subservice organization and incorporated in the design of the system, if operating effectively,*** were those necessary to provide reasonable assurance that the applicable trust services criteria were met, operated effectively throughout the period [*date*] to [*date*].

d. XYZ Service Organization complied with the commitments in its statement of privacy practices throughout the period [*date*] to [*date*] ***if the subservice organization complied*** *with those aspects of such privacy practices that it performed.*

All other report paragraphs are unchanged.

Disclaiming an Opinion When the Service Organization Uses the Carve-Out Method to Present a Subservice Organization

4.39 If the service auditor disclaims an opinion because of matters related to the carved-out subservice organization, such as those described in paragraph 3.38 of this guide (for example, because the subservice organization performs important control procedures that are necessary for the service organization to meet the applicable trust services criteria), the service auditor's report should not identify the procedures that were performed or include statements describing the characteristics of a service auditor's engagement because to do so might overshadow the disclaimer. The service auditor would describe the carve-out using an additional paragraph following the scope paragraph (see the illustration in paragraph 4.37). When disclaiming an opinion in such circumstances, the service auditor would add an explanatory paragraph to the service auditor's report that describes the reason for the disclaimer and any deficiencies identified by the service auditor. The following is an example of such a paragraph (new language is shown in boldface italics):

> *The accompanying description of XYZ Service Organization's system indicates that responsibility for important aspects of the personal information life cycle, the controls required for the service organization to meet the trust services criteria applicable to the privacy principle, and performing activities to determine compliance with the commitments in the service organization's statement of privacy practices has been delegated to the subservice organization. Such matters were not included in the scope of our examination.*

When disclaiming an opinion, in addition to adding such an explanatory paragraph to the service auditor's report, the opinion paragraph would be replaced by the following disclaimer of opinion: (new language is shown in boldface italics):

> *Because of the matter described in the preceding paragraph, the scope of our work was not sufficient to enable us to express, and we do not express, an opinion.*

Reporting When the Service Organization Uses the Inclusive Method to Present a Subservice Organization

4.40 Following are modifications to a service auditor's type 2 report for use in engagements in which the service organization uses a subservice organization and presents its description using the inclusive method (new language is shown in boldface italics; deleted language is shown in strikethrough):

Scope

We have examined the attached description titled "XYZ Service Organization's **and ABC Subservice Organization's** Description of the Adaptable Cloud Computing System for the Period January 1, 20X1, to

December 31, 20X1" (the description) and the suitability of the design and operating effectiveness of controls to meet the criteria for the security, availability, processing integrity, and confidentiality principles set forth in TSP section 100, *Trust Services Principles, Criteria, and Illustrations for Security, Availability, Processing Integrity, Confidentiality, and Privacy* (AICPA, *Technical Practice Aids*) (applicable trust services criteria), throughout the period January 1, 20X1, to December 31, 20X1. **ABC Subservice Organization is an independent service organization that provides certain computer processing services to XYZ Service Organization. XYZ Service Organization's description includes a description of those elements of its system provided by ABC Subservice Organization, the controls of which help meet certain applicable trust services criteria.**

*Service organization's **and subservice organization's*** *responsibilities*

XYZ Service Organization **and ABC Subservice Organization** haves provided their attached assertions titled [*title of service organization's assertion*] and [*title of subservice organization assertion*], which is **are** based on the criteria identified in **those** management's assertions. XYZ Service Organization **and ABC Subservice Organization** is **are** responsible for (1) preparing the description and the assertions; (2) the completeness, accuracy, and method of presentation of both the description and assertions; (3) providing the services covered by the description; (4) specifying the controls that meet the applicable trust services criteria and stating them in the description; and (5) designing, implementing, and documenting the controls to meet the applicable trust services criteria.

Service auditor's responsibilities

Our responsibility is to express an opinion on the fairness of the presentation of the description based on the description criteria set forth in XYZ Service Organization's **and ABC Subservice Organization's** assertions and on the suitability of the design and operating effectiveness of the controls to meet the applicable trust services criteria, based on our examination. We conducted our examination in accordance with attestation standards established by the American Institute of Certified Public Accountants. Those standards require that we plan and perform our examination to obtain reasonable assurance about whether, in all material respects, (1) the description is fairly presented based on the description criteria, and (2) the controls were suitably designed and operating effectively to meet the applicable trust services criteria throughout the period [*date*] to [*date*].

Inherent limitations

Because of their nature and inherent limitations, controls at a service organization **or subservice organization** may not always operate effectively to meet the applicable trust services criteria. Also, the projection to the future of any evaluation of the fairness of the presentation of the description or conclusions about the suitability of the design or operating effectiveness of the controls to meet the applicable trust services criteria is subject to the risks that the system may change or that controls at a service organization **or subservice organization** may become inadequate or fail.

Opinion

In our opinion, in all material respects, based on the criteria identified in XYZ Service Organization's **and ABC Subservice Organization's** assertion*s*

 a. the description fairly presents XYZ Service Organization's [*type or name of*] system **and the elements of the system provided by ABC Subservice Organization** that ~~was~~ **were** designed and implemented throughout the period [*date*] to [*date*].

 b. the controls **of XYZ Service Organization and ABC Subservice Organization** stated in the description were suitably designed to provide reasonable assurance that the applicable trust services criteria would be met if the controls operated effectively throughout the period [*date*] to [*date*].

 c. the controls **of XYZ Service Organization and ABC Subservice Organization** that were tested, which were those necessary to provide reasonable assurance that the applicable trust services criteria were met, operated effectively throughout the period from [*date*] to [*date*].

Intended use

This report and the description of tests of controls and the results thereof are intended solely for the information and use of XYZ Service Organization **and ABC Subservice Organization**; user entities of XYZ Service Organization's [*type or name of*] system; and those prospective user entities, independent auditors, and practitioners providing services to such user entities and regulators who have sufficient knowledge and understanding of

- the nature of the service provided by the service organization.

- how the service organization's system interacts with user entities, subservice organizations, and other parties.

- internal control and its limitations.

- complementary user-entity controls and how they interact with related controls at the service organization **and subservice organization** to meet the applicable trust services criteria.

- the applicable trust services criteria.

- the risks that may threaten the achievement of the applicable trust services criteria and how controls address those risks.

This report is not intended to be and should not be used by anyone other than these specified parties.

Intended Users of the Report

4.41 Paragraph .79 of AT section 101, *Attest Engagements* (AICPA, *Professional Standards*), in part, includes the following discussion of the circumstances in which a report is intended solely for the information and use of specified parties:

The need for restriction on the use of a report may result from a number of circumstances, including the purpose of the report, the criteria used in preparation of the subject matter, the extent to which the procedures performed are known or understood, and the potential for the report to be misunderstood when taken out of the context in which it was intended to be used.

4.42 SOC 2 reports have the potential to be misunderstood when taken out of the context in which they were intended to be used. Accordingly, the service auditor's report should include a statement indicating that the report is intended solely for the information and use of management of the service organization and other specified parties who have sufficient knowledge and understanding of the following:

- The nature of the service provided by the service organization
- How the service organization's system interacts with user entities, subservice organizations, and other parties
- Internal control and its limitations
- Complementary user-entity controls and how they interact with related controls at the service organization to meet the applicable trust services criteria
- The applicable trust services criteria
- The risks that may threaten the achievement of the applicable trust services criteria and how controls address those risks

User entities commonly are specified parties. However, in some instances (for example, when the report is intended for use by a regulator), user entities may not be a specified party. If the service organization distributes the report for general marketing purposes, a greater likelihood exists that some users of the report will not have the required knowledge and may misunderstand the report.

4.43 Report users who are most likely to have such knowledge include management of the service organization; management of the user entities; practitioners evaluating or reporting on controls at a user entity; regulators; and others performing services related to controls at the service organization, such as a service auditor reporting on controls at a user entity that is also a service provider to other user entities.

4.44 Management of a prospective user entity may need to obtain an understanding of a service organization's system related to security, availability, processing integrity, confidentiality, or privacy and the historic operating effectiveness of controls at the service organization, either as part of its vendor selection process or to comply with regulatory requirements for vendor acceptance. To understand and make appropriate use of a SOC 2 report, management of a prospective user entity will need the knowledge and understanding identified in paragraph 4.42. When management of a prospective user entity has such knowledge, a SOC 2 report is likely to be helpful to management in evaluating the service organization's system and controls. Accordingly, management of a prospective user entity that has such knowledge would be an appropriate user of a SOC 2 report. Conversely, management of a prospective user entity that does not have such knowledge is unlikely to be an appropriate user of such a report. When certain prospective user entities are intended users of the report, the service auditor's identification of the intended users of the report should include the knowledge and understanding identified in paragraph 4.42.

Illustrative Type 2 Reports

4.45 Although this guide specifies the information to be included in a description of a service organization's system, it is not specific about the format for these reports. Service organizations and service auditors may organize and present the required information in a variety of formats.

4.46 Appendix C, "Illustrative Management Assertions and Related Service Auditor's Reports on Controls at a Service Organization Relevant to Security, Availability, Processing Integrity, Confidentiality, and Privacy," of this guide contains two examples of type 2 reports. These reports illustrate the following:

- A type 2 report on controls at a service organization relevant to security, availability, processing integrity, and confidentiality
- A type 2 report on controls at a service organization relevant to privacy

Appendix A

Information for Management of a Service Organization

Introduction and Background

Many entities function more efficiently and profitably by outsourcing tasks or entire functions to other organizations (service organizations) that have the personnel, expertise, equipment, or technology to accomplish these tasks or functions. Many of these service organizations collect, process, transmit, store, organize, maintain, and dispose of information for other entities. Entities that use service organizations are known as *user entities*. Examples of the services provided by service organizations include the following:

- *Cloud computing.* Providing on-demand access to a shared pool of configurable computing resources (for example, networks, servers, storage, and applications). Additional information about cloud computing is presented in appendix E, "Reporting on Controls at a Cloud Computing Service Organization."

- *Managed security.* Managing access to networks and computing systems for user entities (for example, granting access to a system and preventing, or detecting and mitigating, system intrusion).

- *Financial services customer accounting.* Processing financial transactions on behalf of customers of a bank or investment company. Examples of this service are processing customer securities transactions, maintaining customer account records, providing customers with confirmations of transactions and statements, and providing these and related customer services through the Internet.

- *Customer support.* Providing customers of user entities with online or telephonic postsales support and service management. Examples of these services are warranty inquiries and investigating and responding to customer complaints.

- *Sales force automation.* Providing and maintaining software to automate business tasks for user entities that have a sales force. Examples of such tasks are order processing, information sharing, order tracking, contact management, customer management, sales forecast analysis, and employee performance evaluation.

- *Health care claims management and processing.* Providing medical providers, employers, and insured parties of employers with systems that enable medical records and related health insurance claims to be processed securely and confidentially.

- *Enterprise IT outsourcing services.* Managing, operating, and maintaining user entities' IT data centers, infrastructure, and application systems and related functions that support IT activities, such as network, production, security, change management, hardware, and environmental control activities.

One of the critical roles of management and those charged with governance in any entity is to identify and assess risks to the entity and address those risks through effective internal control. When an entity outsources tasks or functions to a service organization and becomes a user entity, it replaces many of the risks associated with performing those tasks or functions with risks associated with outsourcing, particularly risks related to how the service organization performs the tasks or functions and how that may affect the user entity's compliance with requirements. Although a task or function is outsourced, management of the user entity retains responsibility for managing these risks and needs to monitor the services provided by the service organization.

To carry out its responsibilities related to the outsourced tasks or functions, management of a user entity needs information about the system by which the service organization provides services, including the service organization's controls[1] over that system. User-entity management may also wish to obtain assurance that the system information provided by the service organization is accurate and that the service organization actually operates in accordance with that information.

To obtain assurance, user entities often ask the service organization for a CPA's report on the service organization's system. Historically, such requests have focused on controls at the service organization that affect user entities' financial reporting. However, user entities are now requesting reports that address the security, availability, or processing integrity of the system or the confidentiality or privacy of the information processed by the system. In this document, these attributes of a system are referred to as *principles*.

The AICPA is alerting CPAs to the various types of engagements that a CPA may perform when reporting on controls at a service organization and has identified these reports as service organization controls (SOC) reports. The objective of this effort is to help CPAs select the appropriate reporting option depending on the subject matter addressed by the controls. The following three types of SOC reports are designed to help CPAs meet specific service organization and user entity needs:

- *SOC 1 report.* These reports are intended to meet the needs of entities that use service organizations (user entities) and the CPAs who audit the user entities' financial statements (user auditors) when evaluating the effect of controls at the service organization on the user entities' financial statements. User auditors use these reports to plan and perform audits of the user entities' financial statements. SOC 1 engagements are performed under Statement on Standards for Attestation Engagements (SSAE) No. 16, *Reporting on Controls at a Service Organization* (AICPA, *Professional Standards*, AT sec. 801), and the AICPA Guide *Service Organizations: Applying SSAE No. 16*, Reporting on Controls at a Service Organization.

- *SOC 2 report.* These reports are intended to meet the needs of a broad range of users who need information and assurance about controls at a service organization that affect the security, availability, or processing integrity of the systems that the service organization uses to process users' data or the confidentiality or privacy

---

[1] From a governance and internal control perspective, *controls* are policies and procedures that address risks associated with financial reporting, operations, or compliance and, when operating effectively, enable an entity to meet specified criteria.

of the information processed by these systems. Examples of stakeholders who may need these reports are management or those charged with governance of the user entities and service organization, customers of the service organization, regulators, business partners, suppliers, and others who have an understanding of the service organization and its controls. These reports include a detailed description of the service organization's system; the criteria in TSP section 100, *Trust Services Principles, Criteria, and Illustrations for Security, Availability, Processing Integrity, Confidentiality, and Privacy* (AICPA, *Technical Practice Aids*), applicable to the principle being reported on; the controls designed to meet these criteria; a written assertion by management regarding the description and the design and operation of the controls; and a service auditor's report (the letter) in which the service auditor expresses an opinion on whether the description is fairly presented and the controls are suitability designed and operating effectively. The report also includes the service auditor's description of tests performed and results of the tests. These reports can play an important role in the following:

— Vendor management programs[2]

— Internal corporate governance and risk management processes

— Regulatory compliance

These engagements are performed under AT section 101, *Attest Engagements* (AICPA, *Professional Standards*), and the AICPA Guide *Reporting on Controls at a Service Organization Relevant to Security, Availability, Processing Integrity, Confidentiality, or Privacy*.

● *SOC 3 report.* These reports are designed to meet the needs of a wider range of users who need assurance about controls at a service organization that affect the security, availability, or processing integrity of the systems used by a service organization to process users' information, or the confidentiality or privacy of that information, but do not have the need for, or knowledge necessary to effectively use, a SOC 2 report. These reports comprise a written assertion by management regarding the suitability of the design and operation of the controls implemented, a CPA's report on the suitability of the design and operating effectiveness of the controls, and a description of the system and its boundaries. This description generally is brief and does not include the detail provided in a SOC 2 system description. The criteria for evaluating the controls are the criteria in TSP section 100 that are relevant to the principle being reported on (the same criteria as in a SOC 2 report). Because they are general-use reports, SOC 3 reports can be freely distributed or posted on a website. If the report is unqualified, the service organization is eligible to display on its website the SysTrust for Service Organizations seal. For more information

---

[2] *Vendor management*, in this context, is a user entity's management of the services provided by a service organization.

about the SysTrust for Service Organization seal program, go to www.webtrust.org.

The Trust Service Principles

The following are the five attributes of a reliable system,[3] which are also referred as the *trust services principles*:

    a. *Security*. The system is protected against unauthorized access (both physical and logical).

    b. *Availability*. The system is available for operation and use as committed or agreed.

    c. *Processing integrity*. System processing is complete, accurate, timely, and authorized.

    d. *Confidentiality*. Information designated as confidential is protected as committed or agreed.

    e. *Privacy*. Personal information[4] is collected, used, retained, disclosed, and disposed of in conformity with the commitments in the entity's privacy notice and criteria set forth in *Generally Accepted Privacy Principles* issued jointly by the AICPA and the Canadian Institute of Chartered Accountants.

In a SOC 2 engagement, management of the service organization selects the trust services principle(s) that will be covered by the SOC 2 report. The trust services criteria for the principle(s) covered by the report are referred to as the *applicable trust services criteria*.

Service organization management implements controls over its systems to prevent adverse events from occurring or detect such events as errors, privacy breaches, and theft or loss of information. For example, a control that terminates access to a system after three unsuccessful login attempts is designed to prevent unauthorized access to the system. Management of the service organization may engage a CPA to report on the design and operating effectiveness of controls over its systems. Controls that are suitably designed are able to meet the criteria they were designed to meet if they operate effectively. Controls that operate effectively actually do meet the criteria they were designed to meet over a period of time.

This guide provides guidance to a service auditor examining and reporting on the fairness of the presentation of a description of a service organization's system; the suitability of the design of the service organization's controls over the system as they relate to one or more of the trust services principles; and in certain reports, the operating effectiveness of those controls. The remainder of this appendix is intended to

    • assist management of a service organization in preparing its description of the service organization's system, which serves as the basis for a SOC 2 examination engagement.

---

[3] A *reliable system* is defined in TSP section 100, *Trust Services Principles, Criteria, and Illustrations for Security, Availability, Processing Integrity, Confidentiality, and Privacy* (AICPA, *Technical Practice Aids*), as a system that is capable of operating without material error, fault, or failure during a specified period in a specified environment.

[4] *Personal information* (sometimes referred to as *personally identifiable information*) is information that is about, or can be related to, an identifiable individual.

- familiarize management with its responsibilities when it engages a service auditor to perform a SOC 2 engagement.

This appendix is not intended to provide guidance to

- management of a service organization in preparing the description of a service organization's system for a SOC 1 or SOC 3 report.
- management of a user entity in assessing a service organization's controls that are likely to be relevant to user entities' internal control over financial reporting.
- auditors of user entities (user auditors) in planning and performing an audit of a user entity's financial statements.

In the remainder of this appendix, references to controls over a system mean controls over a system related to one or more of the trust services principles.

Responsibilities of Management of a Service Organization

In a SOC 2 engagement, management of a service organization is responsible for the following:

- Determining the type of engagement to be performed; which principle(s) will be addressed in the engagement; the scope of the engagement, as discussed in the first paragraph of the "Defining the Scope of the Engagement" section of this appendix; and whether any subservice organizations will be included in, or carved out of, the description and the service auditor's report. (*Subservice organizations* are organizations to which the service organization outsources aspects of the services that it provides.)
- Preparing a description of the service organization's system.
- Providing a written assertion.
- Providing written representations.
- Having a reasonable basis for its assertion.

Determining the Type of Engagement to Be Performed

This guide provides for the following two types of SOC 2 engagements and related reports:

- Report on management's description of a service organization's system and the suitability of the design of controls (referred to as a *type 1 report*)
- Report on management's description of a service organization's system and the suitability of the design and operating effectiveness of controls (referred to as a *type 2 report*)

Both type 1 and type 2 reports include the following:

- Management's description of the service organization's system
- A written assertion by management of the service organization about the matters in the first paragraph of the "Providing a Written Assertion" section of this appendix.

- A service auditor's report that expresses an opinion on the matters in the first paragraph of the "Providing a Written Assertion" section of this appendix.

A type 2 report also contains a description of the service auditor's tests of the controls and the results of the tests, and when the report addresses the privacy principle, a description of the service auditor's tests of the service organization's compliance with the commitments in its statement of privacy practices and the results of those tests.

Management's written assertion is attached to the description of the service organization's system.

A type 1 report, which does not include tests of the operating effectiveness of controls, provides user entities with information that will enable them to understand and assess the design of the controls. However, a type 1 report does not provide sufficient information for user entities to assess the operating effectiveness of the controls. A type 1 report may be useful if the service organization[5]

- has not been in operation for a sufficient length of time to enable the service auditor to gather sufficient appropriate evidence regarding the operating effectiveness of controls.

- has recently made significant changes to the system and related controls and does not have a sufficient history with a stable system to enable a type 2 engagement to be performed.

Defining the Scope of the Engagement

In determining the scope of a SOC 2 engagement, management of a service organization considers the following:

- The services, business units, functional areas, business processes, and activities or applications that will be of interest to users because of concerns regarding compliance with laws or regulations or governance or because the service organization has made commitments to user entities to provide a type 1 or type 2 report.

- The trust services principles that will be covered by the report. Management makes this determination by understanding the needs of report users and the service organization's goals in engaging a service auditor to perform the examination. The engagement may cover one, multiple, or all of the principles.

- The period to be covered by the description and report (for a type 1 report, this would be the as of date of the description and report).

- Whether controls at subservice organizations are relevant to meeting one or more of the applicable trust services criteria. (Subservice organizations may be separate entities from the service organization or entities related to the service organization.)

---

[5] A user of a type 1 report may misunderstand the nature of the engagement and incorrectly assume that controls are operating effectively or that the entity has complied with the practices in its privacy notice, even though the service auditor has not provided such an opinion or performed sufficient procedures to express such an opinion. When the report user is a regulatory agency or body, this misunderstanding may result in regulatory compliance risk, particularly in a report that addresses the privacy principle.

To increase the likelihood that the description and service auditor's report will be useful to report users, management of the service organization may wish to discuss with user entities matters such as the services, trust services principles, and period or as of date to be covered by the description and service auditor's report.

If a service organization uses a subservice organization, the description of the service organization's system may either (a) include the subservice organization's services by using the inclusive method or (b) exclude the subservice organization's services by using the carve-out method.

When the carve-out method is used, management's description of the service organization's system identifies the nature of the services and functions performed by the subservice organization and the types of controls that management expects to be implemented at the subservice organization but excludes details of the subservice organization's system and controls.

A service organization's description prepared using the carve-out method generally is most useful if the services provided by the subservice organization are not extensive or if a type 1 or type 2 report that meets the needs of user entities is available from the subservice organization.

When the inclusive method is used, management's description of the service organization's system includes a description of the nature of the services and functions performed by the subservice organization, as well the applicable trust services criteria and controls implemented by the subservice organization. Controls of the service organization are presented separately from those of the subservice organization.

Although the inclusive method provides more information for user entities, it may not be appropriate or feasible in all circumstances. In determining which approach to use, the service organization considers (a) the nature and extent of the information about the subservice organization that user entities may need and (b) the practical difficulties entailed in implementing the inclusive method.

The inclusive method is difficult to implement in certain circumstances. The approach entails extensive planning and communication among the service auditor, the service organization, and the subservice organization. If a service organization wishes to use the inclusive method of presentation, matters such as the following generally will need to be coordinated by all the parties involved, preferably in advance:

- The scope of the description and the timing of the examination and tests of controls
- Responsibility for preparing the section of the description that relates to the services provided by the subservice organization
- The content of the subservice organization's written representations and the members of the subservice organization's management who will be responsible for the written representations
- An agreement regarding access to the subservice organization's premises, personnel, and systems
- Fees
- Identification of the parties for whom use of the report is intended

These issues become more complex if multiple subservice organizations are involved, and the inclusive method is used. The inclusive approach is facilitated if the service organization and subservice organization are related parties or have a contractual relationship that provides for inclusive reports and visits by service auditors.

If more than one subservice organization is relevant to user entities, management of the service organization may use the inclusive method for one or more subservice organizations and the carve-out method for one or more of the other subservice organizations.

If the service organization uses the inclusive method, the service organization would obtain a written assertion from management of the subservice organization covering the subservice organization's services. That assertion would also be attached to the description of the service organization's system. If management of the subservice organization will not provide a written assertion, the service organization cannot use the inclusive method but may instead be able to use the carve-out method.

If the service organization's controls and monitoring of the activities of a subservice organization are sufficient to meet the applicable trust services criteria, the controls at the subservice organization are not necessary to meet those criteria. In such instances, the service organization's assertion is based solely on controls at the service organization, and consequently, neither the inclusive nor carve-out method is applicable. In these situations, the description need not describe the subservice organization's activities, unless such information is needed to help users understand the service organization's system.

Preparing the Description of the Service Organization's System

Management of a service organization is responsible for preparing the description, including the completeness, accuracy, and method of presentation of the description. No one particular format for the description is prescribed, and the extent of the description may vary, depending on the size and complexity of the service organization and its activities. The description may be presented using various formats, such as narratives, flowcharts, tables, and graphics, but should meet the criteria set forth in the "Criteria for Management's Description of the Service Organization's System" section of this appendix.

Appendix B, "Trust Services Principles and Criteria for Security, Availability, Processing Integrity, Confidentiality, and Privacy," of this guide contains the control criteria for each of the trust services principles. All the criteria related to the trust services principle(s) being reported on (applicable trust services criteria) should be included in management's description. For example, if a service auditor is reporting on the design and operating effectiveness of controls at a service organization relevant to the security of user entities' information, all the control criteria related to security should be addressed by the description. If the description does not describe controls for one or more control criteria, the description should include an explanation of why such criteria are not addressed by a control. Omission of controls related to one or more of the applicable trust services criteria would be appropriate if the omitted criteria are not applicable to the services provided by the service organization.

For example, in an engagement to report on the privacy principle in which personal information is collected from individuals by user entities, not the service organization, it would be appropriate to omit controls for the criteria related to collection and describe the reason for such omission. However, for certain criteria, a policy prohibiting certain activities is not sufficient to render a criterion not applicable. For example, in a SOC 2 report that addresses the privacy principle, it would not be appropriate for a service organization to omit controls for the criteria related to disclosure of personal information to third parties based only on the fact that the service organization's policies forbid such disclosure. Such policies would need to be suitably designed, implemented, and operating effectively to conclude that they prevent such disclosure.

The description need not address every aspect of the service organization's system or the services provided to user entities. Certain aspects of the services provided may not be relevant to user entities or may be beyond the scope of the engagement. For example, a service organization's processes related to availability are not likely to be relevant in an engagement that addresses only the security principle. Similarly, although the description should include procedures within both manual and automated systems by which services are provided, it need not necessarily include every step in the process.

The description needs to meet certain criteria in order to be fairly presented. These criteria are set forth in the "Criteria for Management's Description of the Service Organization's System" section of this appendix. As a part of the SOC 2 engagement, the service auditor evaluates the fairness of the presentation of the description using these criteria.

Providing a Written Assertion

Management of the service organization prepares a written assertion that is to be attached to the description of the service organization's system. In its assertion, management confirms, to the best of its knowledge and belief, that

    a. management's description of the service organization's system fairly presents the service organization's system that was designed and implemented throughout the specified period, based on the criteria in the "Criteria for Management's Description of the Service Organization's System" section of this appendix.

    b. the controls stated in management's description of the service organization's system were suitably designed throughout the specified period to meet the applicable trust services criteria.

    c. the controls stated in management's description of the service organization's system operated effectively throughout the specified period to meet the applicable trust services criteria (type 2 report only).

    d. when management's description of the service organization's system includes controls over privacy, the service organization complied with the commitments in its statement of privacy practices throughout the specified period (type 2 report only).

Management of the service organization needs to have a reasonable basis for its written assertion, which typically is based on management's monitoring activities and other procedures.

Management's monitoring activities may provide a portion of the basis for making its assertion regarding the design and operating effectiveness of controls or may be a sufficient basis on its own. Monitoring of controls is a process to assess the effectiveness of internal control performance over time. It involves assessing the effectiveness of controls on a timely basis, identifying and reporting deficiencies to appropriate individuals within the service organization, and taking necessary corrective actions. Management accomplishes monitoring of controls through ongoing activities, separate evaluations, or a combination of the two. Ongoing monitoring activities are often built into the normal recurring activities of an entity and include regular management and supervisory activities. Internal auditors or personnel performing similar functions may contribute to the monitoring of a service organization's activities. Monitoring activities may also include using information communicated by external parties, such as customer complaints and regulator comments, which may indicate problems or highlight areas in need of improvement. The greater the degree and effectiveness of ongoing monitoring, the less need for separate evaluations. Usually, some combination of ongoing monitoring and separate evaluations will help ensure that internal control maintains its effectiveness over time. The service auditor's report on controls is not a substitute for the service organization's own processes that provide a reasonable basis for its assertion.

When monitoring does not provide a basis for management's assertion regarding the design and operating effectiveness of controls, service organization management may need to perform its own tests of the service organization's controls.

Additional Management Responsibilities

The following are some of the additional responsibilities that management of the service organization will have throughout the engagement:

- Providing access to all information, such as information in records, documentation, service level agreements, internal audit reports and other reports that management is aware of, that is relevant to the description of the service organization's system or the design and operating effectiveness of controls and management's assertion.

- Providing additional information that the service auditor may request from management for the purpose of the examination engagement.

- Providing unrestricted access to personnel within the service organization from whom the service auditor determines it is necessary to obtain evidence relevant to the service auditor's engagement.

- Disclosing to the service auditor any deficiencies in the design of controls of which management is aware.

- Disclosing to the service auditor all instances of which management is aware when controls have not operated with sufficient effectiveness to meet the applicable trust services criteria.

- Disclosing to the service auditor incidents of noncompliance with laws and regulations, fraud, or uncorrected errors attributable to management or other service organization personnel that are clearly not trivial and may affect one or more user entities and whether such incidents have been communicated appropriately to affected user entities.

- Providing written representations at the conclusion of the engagement. When the inclusive method is used, management of the service organization and subservice organization are responsible for providing separate representations. In its representations, management includes statements that

— reaffirm its written assertion attached to the description.

— the service organization has provided the service auditor with all relevant information and the access agreed to.

— the service organization has disclosed to the service auditor any of the following of which it is aware:

- Instances of noncompliance with laws or regulations or uncorrected errors attributable to the service organization that may affect one or more user entities.

- Knowledge of any actual, suspected, or alleged intentional acts by management of the service organization or its employees that could adversely affect the fairness of the presentation of management's description of the service organization's system or whether the controls stated in the description were suitably designed and operating effectively to meet the applicable trust services criteria.

- Deficiencies in the design of controls.

- Instances when controls have not operated as described.

- Any events subsequent to the period covered by management's description of the service organization's system up to the date of the service auditor's report that could have a significant effect on management's assertion or the fact that no such subsequent events have occurred.

Criteria for Management's Description of the Service Organization's System

The criteria for determining whether the description of the service organization's system is fairly presented are as follows:

a. The description contains the following information:

i. The types of services provided

ii. The components of the system used to provide the services, which are the following:

(1) *Infrastructure.* The physical and hardware components of a system (facilities, equipment, and networks).

(2) *Software.* The programs and operating software of a system (systems, applications, and utilities).

(3) *People.* The personnel involved in the operation and use of a system (developers, operators, users, and managers).

(4) *Procedures.* The automated and manual procedures involved in the operation of a system.

    (5) *Data*. The information used and supported by a system (transaction streams, files, databases, and tables).

iii. The boundaries of the system covered by the description

iv. How the service organization's system captures and addresses significant events and conditions[6]

v. The process used to prepare and deliver reports and other information to user entities and other parties

vi. For information provided to, or received from, subservice organizations and other parties

    (1) how the information is provided or received and the role of the subservice organizations and other parties

    (2) the procedures that the service organization performs to determine that such information and its processing, maintenance, and storage are subject to appropriate controls

vii. For each principle being reported on, the related criteria in TSP section 100 (applicable trust services criteria) and the related controls designed to meet those criteria, including, as applicable, the following:

    (1) Complementary user-entity controls contemplated in the design of the service organization's system

    (2) When the inclusive method is used to present a subservice organization, controls at the subservice organization

viii. If the service organization presents the subservice organization using the carve-out method

    (1) the nature of the services provided by the subservice organization

    (2) any aspects of the personal information life cycle for which responsibility has been delegated to the subservice organization

    (3) each of the applicable trust services criteria that are intended to be met by controls at the subservice organization, alone or in combination with controls at the service organization, and the types of controls expected to be implemented at carved-out subservice organizations to meet those criteria

    (4) when the report addresses the privacy principle, the types of activities that the subservice organization would need to perform to comply with the service organization's privacy commitments

---

[6] For example, the setup of access rights for new users of the system.

ix. Identifying any applicable trust services criteria that are not addressed by a control at the service organization or subservice organization and the reasons therefore

x. Other aspects of the service organization's control environment, risk assessment process, information and communication systems, and monitoring of controls that are relevant to the services provided and the applicable trust services criteria

xi. In the case of a type 2 report, relevant details of changes to the service organization's system during the period covered by the description

b. The description does not omit or distort information relevant to the service organization's system while acknowledging that the description is prepared to meet the common needs of a broad range of users and may not, therefore, include every aspect of the system that each individual user may consider important to his or her own particular needs.

c. For engagements to report on the privacy principle

i. the types of personal information collected from individuals or obtained from user entities or other parties[7] and how such information is collected and, if collected by user entities, how it is obtained by the service organization.

ii. the process for (1) identifying specific requirements in agreements with user entities and laws and regulations applicable to the personal information and (2) implementing controls and practices to meet those requirements.

iii. if the service organization provides the privacy notice to individuals about whom personal information is collected, used, retained, disclosed, and disposed of or anonymized, the privacy notice prepared in conformity with the relevant criteria for a privacy notice set forth in TSP section 100.

iv. if the service organization presents the subservice organization using the carve-out method

(1) any aspects of the personal information life cycle for which responsibility has been delegated to the subservice organization and

(2) the types of activities that the subservice organization would need to perform to comply with the service organization's privacy commitments.

v. if the user entities, rather than the service organization, are responsible for providing the privacy notice to individuals, a statement regarding how the privacy notice is communicated to individuals, that the user entities are responsible for communicating such notice to individuals, and that the service organization is responsible for communicating its privacy practices to the user entities in its

---

[7] An example of an entity that collects personal information from user entities is a credit-reporting bureau that maintains information about the creditworthiness of individuals.

statement of privacy practices, which includes the following information:

(1) A summary of the significant privacy and related security requirements common to most agreements between the service organization and its user entities and any requirements in a particular user-entity's agreement that the service organization meets for all or most user entities

(2) A summary of the significant privacy and related security requirements mandated by law, regulation, industry, or market requirements that are not included in user-entity agreements but that the service organization meets for all or most user entities

(3) The purposes, uses, and disclosures of personal information as permitted by user-entity agreements and beyond those permitted by such agreements but not prohibited by such agreements and the service organization's commitments regarding the purpose, use, and disclosure of personal information that are prohibited by such agreements

(4) A statement that the information will be retained for a period no longer than necessary to fulfill the stated purposes or contractual requirements or for the period required by law or regulation, as applicable, or a statement describing other retention practices

(5) A statement that the information will be disposed of in a manner that prevents loss, theft, misuse, or unauthorized access to the information

(6) If applicable, how the service organization supports any process permitted by user entities for individuals to obtain access to their information to review, update, or correct it

(7) If applicable, a description of the process to determine that personal information is accurate and complete and how the service organization implements correction processes permitted by user entities

(8) If applicable, how inquiries, complaints, and disputes from individuals (whether directly from the individual or indirectly through user entities) regarding their personal information are handled by the service organization

(9) A statement regarding the existence of a written security program and what industry or other standards it is based on

(10) Other relevant information related to privacy practices deemed appropriate for user entities by the service organization

    vi. if the user entities, rather than the service organization, are responsible for providing the privacy notice to individuals, the service organization's statement of privacy practices.

Appendix B

Trust Services Principles and Criteria for Security, Availability, Processing Integrity, Confidentiality, and Privacy

TSP Section 100 Principles and Criteria

Security Principle and Criteria Table

The system is protected against unauthorized access (both physical and logical)

	Criteria
1.0	**Policies: The entity defines and documents its policies for the security of its system.**
1.1	The entity's security policies are established and periodically reviewed and approved by a designated individual or group.
1.2	The entity's security policies include, but may not be limited to, the following matters:

    a. Identifying and documenting the security requirements of authorized users

    b. Classifying data based on its criticality and sensitivity and that classification is used to define protection requirements, access rights and access restrictions, and retention and destruction requirements

    c. Assessing risks on a periodic basis

    d. Preventing unauthorized access

    e. Adding new users, modifying the access levels of existing users, and removing users who no longer need access

    f. Assigning responsibility and accountability for system security

    g. Assigning responsibility and accountability for system changes and maintenance

    h. Testing, evaluating, and authorizing system components before implementation

    i. Addressing how complaints and requests relating to security issues are resolved

    j. Identifying and mitigating security breaches and other incidents

    k. Providing for training and other resources to support its system security policies

    l. Providing for the handling of exceptions and situations not specifically addressed in its system security policies

(continued)

Criteria

m. Providing for the identification of and consistency with applicable laws and regulations, defined commitments, service-level agreements, and other contractual requirements

n. Providing for sharing information with third parties

1.3　Responsibility and accountability for developing and maintaining the entity's system security policies, and changes and updates to those policies, are assigned.

2.0　Communications: The entity communicates its defined system security policies to responsible parties and authorized users.

2.1　The entity has prepared an objective description of the system and its boundaries and communicated such description to authorized users.

2.2　The security obligations of users and the entity's security commitments to users are communicated to authorized users.

2.3　Responsibility and accountability for the entity's system security policies and changes and updates to those policies are communicated to entity personnel responsible for implementing them.

2.4　The process for informing the entity about breaches of the system security and for submitting complaints is communicated to authorized users.

2.5　Changes that may affect system security are communicated to management and users who will be affected.

3.0　Procedures: The entity placed in operation procedures to achieve its documented system security objectives in accordance with its defined policies.

3.1　Procedures exist to (1) identify potential threats of disruption to systems operation that would impair system security commitments and (2) assess the risks associated with the identified threats.

3.2　Procedures exist to restrict logical access to the defined system including, but not limited to, the following matters:

a. Logical access security measures to restrict access to information resources not deemed to be public.

b. Identification and authentication of users.

c. Registration and authorization of new users.

d. The process to make changes and updates to user profiles.

e. Distribution of output restricted to authorized users.

f. Restriction of access to offline storage, backup data, systems, and media.

g. Restriction of access to system configurations, superuser functionality, master passwords, powerful utilities, and security devices (for example, firewalls).

Criteria

3.3	Procedures exist to restrict physical access to the defined system including, but not limited to, facilities, backup media, and other system components such as firewalls, routers, and servers.
3.4	Procedures exist to protect against unauthorized access to system resources.
3.5	Procedures exist to protect against infection by computer viruses, malicious code, and unauthorized software.
3.6	Encryption or other equivalent security techniques are used to protect user authentication information and the corresponding session transmitted over the Internet or other public networks.
Criteria related to execution and incident management used to achieve objectives	
3.7	Procedures exist to identify, report, and act upon system security breaches and other incidents.
Criteria related to the system components used to achieve the objectives	
3.8	Procedures exist to classify data in accordance with classification policies and periodically monitor and update such classifications as necessary
3.9	Procedures exist to provide that issues of noncompliance with security policies are promptly addressed and that corrective measures are taken on a timely basis.
3.10	Design, acquisition, implementation, configuration, modification, and management of infrastructure and software are consistent with defined system security policies to enable authorized access and to prevent unauthorized access.
3.11	Procedures exist to provide that personnel responsible for the design, development, implementation, and operation of systems affecting security have the qualifications and resources to fulfill their responsibilities.
Change management-related criteria applicable to the system's security	
3.12	Procedures exist to maintain system components, including configurations consistent with the defined system security policies.
3.13	Procedures exist to provide that only authorized, tested, and documented changes are made to the system.
3.14	Procedures exist to provide that emergency changes are documented and authorized timely.
4.0	**Monitoring: The entity monitors the system and takes action to maintain compliance with its defined system security policies.**

(continued)

	Criteria
4.1	The entity's system security is periodically reviewed and compared with the defined system security policies.
4.2	There is a process to identify and address potential impairments to the entity's ongoing ability to achieve its objectives in accordance with its defined system security policies.
4.3	Environmental, regulatory, and technological changes are monitored and their effect on system security is assessed on a timely basis and policies are updated for that assessment.

Availability Principle and Criteria Table

The system is available for operation and use as committed or agreed.

	Criteria
1.0	**Policies: The entity defines and documents its policies for the availability of its system.**
1.1	The entity's system availability and related security policies are established and periodically reviewed and approved by a designated individual or group.
1.2	The entity's system availability and related security policies include, but may not be limited to, the following matters:

    a. Identifying and documenting the system availability and related security requirements of authorized users.

    b. Classifying data based on its criticality and sensitivity and that classification is used to define protection requirements, access rights and access restrictions, and retention and destruction requirements

    c. Assessing risks on a periodic basis

    d. Preventing unauthorized access.

    e. Adding new users, modifying the access levels of existing users, and removing users who no longer need access.

    f. Assigning responsibility and accountability for system availability and related security.

    g. Assigning responsibility and accountability for system changes and maintenance.

    h. Testing, evaluating, and authorizing system components before implementation.

    i. Addressing how complaints and requests relating to system availability and related security issues are resolved.

    j. Identifying and mitigating system availability and related security breaches and other incidents.

    k. Providing for training and other resources to support its system availability and related security policies.

Criteria

    l. Providing for the handling of exceptions and situations not specifically addressed in its system availability and related security policies.

    m. Providing for the identification of and consistency with, applicable laws and regulations, defined commitments, service-level agreements, and other contractual requirements.

    n. Recovering and continuing service in accordance with documented customer commitments or other agreements.

    o. Monitoring system capacity to achieve customer commitments or other agreements regarding availability

1.3   Responsibility and accountability for developing and maintaining the entity's system availability and related security policies, and changes and updates to those policies, are assigned.

2.0   Communications: The entity communicates the defined system availability policies to responsible parties and authorized users.

2.1   The entity has prepared an objective description of the system and its boundaries and communicated such description to authorized users.

2.2   The availability and related security obligations of users and the entity's availability and related security commitments to users are communicated to authorized users.

2.3   Responsibility and accountability for the entity's system availability and related security policies and changes and updates to those policies are communicated to entity personnel responsible for implementing them.

2.4   The process for informing the entity about system availability issues and breaches of system security and for submitting complaints is communicated to authorized users.

2.5   Changes that may affect system availability and system security are communicated to management and users who will be affected.

3.0   Procedures: The entity placed in operation procedures to achieve its documented system availability objectives in accordance with its defined policies.

3.1   Procedures exist to (1) identify potential threats of disruptions to systems operation that would impair system availability commitments and (2) assess the risks associated with the identified threats.

3.2   Measures to prevent or mitigate threats have been implemented consistent with the risk assessment when commercially practicable.

3.3   Procedures exist to provide for backup, offsite storage, restoration, and disaster recovery consistent with the entity's defined system availability and related security policies.

3.4   Procedures exist to provide for the integrity of backup data and systems maintained to support the entity's defined system availability and related security policies.

(continued)

Criteria

Security-related criteria relevant to the system's availability

3.5   Procedures exist to restrict logical access to the defined system including, but not limited to, the following matters:

    a. Logical access security measures to restrict access to information resources not deemed to be public.

    b. Identification and authentication of users.

    c. Registration and authorization of new users.

    d. The process to make changes and updates to user profiles.

    e. Restriction of access to offline storage, backup data, systems and media.

    f. Restriction of access to system configurations, superuser functionality, master passwords, powerful utilities, and security devices (for example, firewalls).

3.6   Procedures exist to restrict physical access to the defined system including, but not limited to, facilities, backup media, and other system components such as firewalls, routers, and servers.

3.7   Procedures exist to protect against unauthorized access to system resources.

3.8   Procedures exist to protect against infection by computer viruses, malicious codes, and unauthorized software.

3.9   Encryption or other equivalent security techniques are used to protect user authentication information and the corresponding session transmitted over the Internet or other public networks.

Criteria related to execution and incident management used to achieve objectives

3.10   Procedures exist to identify, report, and act upon system availability issues and related security breaches and other incidents.

Criteria related to the system components used to achieve the objectives

3.11   Procedures exist to classify data in accordance with classification policies and periodically monitor and update such classifications as necessary.

3.12   Procedures exist to provide that issues of noncompliance with system availability and related security policies are promptly addressed and that corrective measures are taken on a timely basis.

3.13   Design, acquisition, implementation, configuration, modification, and management of infrastructure and software are consistent with defined system availability and related security policies.

3.14   Procedures exist to provide that personnel responsible for the design, development, implementation, and operation of systems affecting availability and security have the qualifications and resources to fulfill their responsibilities.

Criteria

Change management-related criteria applicable to the system's availability

3.15 Procedures exist to maintain system components, including configurations consistent with the defined system availability and related security policies.

3.16 Procedures exist to provide that only authorized, tested, and documented changes are made to the system.

3.17 Procedures exist to provide that emergency changes are documented and authorized (including after-the-fact approval).

4.0 Monitoring: The entity monitors the system and takes action to maintain compliance with its defined system availability policies.

4.1 The entity's system availability and security performance is periodically reviewed and compared with the defined system availability and related security policies.

4.2 There is a process to identify and address potential impairments to the entity's ongoing ability to achieve its objectives in accordance with its defined system availability and related security policies.

4.3 Environmental, regulatory, and technological changes are monitored, and their effect on system availability and security is assessed on a timely basis; policies are updated for that assessment.

Processing Integrity Principle and Criteria Table

System processing is complete, accurate, timely, and authorized.

Criteria
1.0 Policies: The entity defines and documents its policies for the processing integrity of its system.

1.1 The entity's processing integrity and related security policies are established and periodically reviewed and approved by a designated individual or group.

1.2 The entity's system processing integrity and related security policies include, but may not be limited to, the following matters:

a. Identifying and documenting the system processing integrity and related security requirements of authorized users

b. Classifying data based on their criticality and sensitivity; that classification is used to define protection requirements, access rights and access restrictions, and retention and destruction requirements

c. Assessing risks on a periodic basis

d. Preventing unauthorized access

e. Adding new users, modifying the access levels of existing users, and removing users who no longer need access

(continued)

Criteria

    f. Assigning responsibility and accountability for system processing integrity and related security

    g. Assigning responsibility and accountability for system changes and maintenance

    h. Testing, evaluating, and authorizing system components before implementation

    i. Addressing how complaints and requests relating to system processing integrity and related security issues are resolved

    j. Identifying and mitigating errors and omissions and other system processing integrity and related security breaches and other incidents

    k. Providing for training and other resources to support its system processing integrity and related system security policies

    l. Providing for the handling of exceptions and situations not specifically addressed in its system processing integrity and related system security policies

    m. Providing for the identification of and consistency with applicable laws and regulations, defined commitments, service-level agreements, and other contractual requirements

1.3   Responsibility and accountability for developing and maintaining entity's system processing integrity and related system security policies; changes, updates, and exceptions to those policies are assigned.

2.0   Communications: The entity communicates its documented system processing integrity policies to responsible parties and authorized users.

2.1   The entity has prepared an objective description of the system and its boundaries and communicated such description to authorized users.

If the system is an e-commerce system, additional information provided on its website includes, but may not be limited to, the following matters:

    a. Descriptive information about the nature of the goods or services that will be provided, including, where appropriate,

        — condition of goods (whether they are new, used, or reconditioned).

        — description of services (or service contract).

        — sources of information (where it was obtained and how it was compiled).

    b. The terms and conditions by which it conducts its e-commerce transactions including, but not limited to, the following matters:

        — Time frame for completion of transactions (*transaction* means fulfillment of orders where goods are being sold and delivery of service where a service is being provided)

        — Time frame and process for informing customers of exceptions to normal processing of orders or service requests

Criteria

- Normal method of delivery of goods or services, including customer options, where applicable

- Payment terms, including customer options, if any

- Electronic settlement practices and related charges to customers

- How customers may cancel recurring charges, if any

- Product return policies and limited liability, where applicable

    c. Where customers can obtain warranty, repair service, and support related to the goods and services purchased on its website.

    d. Procedures for resolution of issues regarding processing integrity. These may relate to any part of a customer's e-commerce transaction, including complaints related to the quality of services and products, accuracy, completeness, and the consequences for failure to resolve such complaints.

2.2   The processing integrity and related security obligations of users and the entity's processing integrity and related security commitments to users are communicated to authorized users.

2.3   Responsibility and accountability for the entity's system processing integrity and related security policies, and changes and updates to those policies, are communicated to entity personnel responsible for implementing them.

2.4   The process for obtaining support and informing the entity about system processing integrity issues, errors and omissions, and breaches of systems security and for submitting complaints is communicated to authorized users.

2.5   Changes that may affect system processing integrity and system security are communicated to management and users who will be affected.

3.0   **Procedures: The entity placed in operation procedures to achieve its documented system processing integrity objectives in accordance with its defined policies.**

3.1   Procedures exist to (1) identify potential threats of disruptions to systems operations that would impair processing integrity commitments and (2) assess the risks associated with the identified threats.

3.2   The procedures related to completeness, accuracy, timeliness, and authorization of inputs are consistent with the documented system processing integrity policies.

    If the system is an e-commerce system, the entity's procedures include, but may not be limited to, the following matters:

    a. The entity checks each request or transaction for accuracy and completeness.

    b. Positive acknowledgment is received from the customer before the transaction is processed.

(continued)

Criteria

3.3 The procedures related to completeness, accuracy, timeliness, and authorization of system processing, including error correction and database management, are consistent with documented system processing integrity policies.

If the system is an e-commerce system, the entity's procedures include, but are not necessarily limited to, the following matters:

a. The correct goods are shipped in the correct quantities in the time frame agreed upon, or services and information are provided to the customer as requested.

b. Transaction exceptions are promptly communicated to the customer.

c. Incoming messages are processed and delivered accurately and completely to the correct IP address.

d. Outgoing messages are processed and delivered accurately and completely to the service provider's (SP's) Internet access point.

e. Messages remain intact while in transit within the confines of the SP's network.

3.4 The procedures related to completeness, accuracy, timeliness, and authorization of outputs are consistent with the documented system processing integrity policies.

If the system is an e-commerce system, the entity's procedures include, but are not necessarily limited to, the following matters:

- The entity displays sales prices and all other costs and fees to the customer before processing the transaction.
- Transactions are billed and electronically settled as agreed.
- Billing or settlement errors are promptly corrected.

3.5 There are procedures to enable tracing of information inputs from their source to their final disposition and vice versa.

Security-related criteria relevant to the system's processing integrity

3.6 Procedures exist to restrict logical access to the defined system including, but not limited to, the following matters:

a. Logical access security measures to access information not deemed to be public

b. Identification and authentication of authorized users

c. Registration and authorization of new users

d. The process to make changes and updates to user profiles

e. Distribution of output restricted to authorized users

f. Restriction of access to offline storage, backup data, systems, and media

g. Restriction of access to system configurations, superuser functionality, master passwords, powerful utilities, and security devices (for example, firewalls)

Criteria

3.7 Procedures exist to restrict physical access to the defined system including, but not limited to, facilities, offline storage media, backup media and systems, and other system components such as firewalls, routers, and servers.

3.8 Procedures exist to protect against unauthorized access to system resources.

3.9 Procedures exist to protect against infection by computer viruses, malicious code, and unauthorized software.

3.10 Encryption or other equivalent security techniques are used to protect user authentication information and the corresponding session transmitted over the Internet or other public networks.

Criteria related to execution and incident management used to achieve objectives

3.11 Procedures exist to identify, report, and act upon system processing integrity issues and related security breaches and other incidents.

Criteria related to the system components used to achieve the objectives

3.12 Procedures exist to classify data in accordance with classification policies and periodically monitor and update such classifications as necessary

3.13 Procedures exist to provide that issues of noncompliance with system processing integrity and related security policies are promptly addressed and that corrective measures are taken on a timely basis.

3.14 Design, acquisition, implementation, configuration, modification, and management of infrastructure and software are consistent with defined processing integrity and related security policies.

3.15 Procedures exist to provide that personnel responsible for the design, development, implementation, and operation of systems affecting processing integrity and security have qualifications and resources to fulfill their responsibilities.

Change management-related criteria applicable to the system's processing integrity

3.16 Procedures exist to maintain system components, including configurations consistent with the defined system processing integrity and related security policies.

3.17 Procedures exist to provide that only authorized, tested, and documented changes are made to the system.

3.18 Procedures exist to provide that emergency changes are documented and authorized (including after-the-fact approval).

Availability-related criteria applicable to the system's processing integrity

(continued)

	Criteria
3.19	Procedures exist to protect the system against potential risks (for example, environmental risks, natural disasters, and routine operational errors and omissions) that might impair system processing integrity.
3.20	Procedures exist to provide for restoration and disaster recovery consistent with the entity's defined processing integrity policies.
3.21	Procedures exist to provide for the completeness, accuracy, and timeliness of backup data and systems.
4.0	**Monitoring: The entity monitors the system and takes action to maintain compliance with the defined system processing integrity policies.**
4.1	System processing integrity and security performance are periodically reviewed and compared with the defined system processing integrity and related security policies.
4.2	There is a process to identify and address potential impairments to the entity's ongoing ability to achieve its objectives in accordance with its defined system processing integrity and related security policies.
4.3	Environmental, regulatory, and technological changes are monitored, their impact on system processing integrity and security is assessed on a timely basis, and policies are updated for that assessment.

Confidentiality Principle and Criteria Table

Information designated as confidential is protected by the system as committed or agreed.

	Criteria
1.0	**Policies: The entity defines and documents its policies related to the system protecting confidential information, as committed or agreed.**
1.1	The entity's system confidentiality and related security policies are established and periodically reviewed and approved by a designated individual or group.
1.2	The entity's policies related to the system's protection of confidential information and security include, but are not limited to, the following matters:
	a. Identifying and documenting the confidentiality and related security requirements of authorized users
	b. Classifying data based on its criticality and sensitivity that is used to define protection requirements, access rights and access restrictions, and retention and destruction requirements
	c. Assessing risk on a periodic basis
	d. Preventing unauthorized access

Criteria

     e. Adding new users, modifying the access levels of existing users, and removing users who no longer need access

     f. Assigning responsibility and accountability for confidentiality and related security

     g. Assigning responsibility and accountability for system changes and maintenance

     h. Testing, evaluating, and authorizing system components before implementation

     i. Addressing how complaints and requests relating to confidentiality and related security issues are resolved

     j. Handling confidentiality and related security breaches and other incidents

     k. Providing for training and other resources to support its system confidentiality and related security policies

     l. Providing for the handling of exceptions and situations not specifically addressed in its system confidentiality and related security policies

     m. Providing for the identification of and consistency with, applicable laws and regulations, defined commitments, service-level agreements, and other contractual requirements

     n. Sharing information with third parties

1.3   Responsibility and accountability for developing and maintaining the entity's system confidentiality and related security policies, and changes and updates to those polices, are assigned.

2.0   Communications: The entity communicates its defined policies related to the system's protection of confidential information to responsible parties and authorized users.

2.1   The entity has prepared an objective description of the system and its boundaries and communicated such description to authorized users.

2.2   The system confidentiality and related security obligations of users and the entity's confidentiality and related security commitments to users are communicated to authorized users before the confidential information is provided. This communication includes, but is not limited to, the following matters:

     a. How information is designated as confidential and ceases to be confidential. The handling, destruction, maintenance, storage, backup, and distribution or transmission of confidential information.

     b. How access to confidential information is authorized and how such authorization is rescinded.

     c. How confidential information is used.

     d. How confidential information is shared.

     e. If information is provided to third parties, disclosures include any limitations on reliance on the third party's confidentiality practices and controls. Lack of such disclosure indicates that the entity is

(continued)

AAG-SOP APP B

Criteria

relying on the third party's confidentiality practices and controls that meet or exceed those of the entity.

    f. Practices to comply with applicable laws and regulations addressing confidentiality.

2.3   Responsibility and accountability for the entity's system confidentiality and related security policies and changes and updates to those policies are communicated to entity personnel responsible for implementing them.

2.4   The process for informing the entity about breaches of confidentiality and system security and for submitting complaints is communicated to authorized users.

2.5   Changes that may affect confidentiality and system security are communicated to management and users who will be affected.

3.0   **Procedures: The entity placed in operation procedures to achieve its documented system confidentiality objectives in accordance with its defined policies.**

3.1   Procedures exist to (1) identify potential threats of disruptions to systems operations that would impair system confidentiality commitments and (2) assess the risks associated with the identified threats.

3.2   The system procedures related to confidentiality of inputs are consistent with the documented confidentiality policies.

3.3   The system procedures related to confidentiality of data processing are consistent with the documented confidentiality policies.

3.4   The system procedures related to confidentiality of outputs are consistent with the documented confidentiality policies.

3.5   The system procedures provide that confidential information is disclosed to parties only in accordance with the entity's defined confidentiality and related security policies.

3.6   The entity has procedures to obtain assurance or representation that the confidentiality policies of third parties to whom information is transferred and upon which the entity relies are in conformity with the entity's defined system confidentiality and related security policies and that the third party is in compliance with its policies.

3.7   In the event that a disclosed confidentiality practice is discontinued or changed to be less restrictive, the entity has procedures to protect confidential information in accordance with the system confidentiality practices in place when such information was received, or obtains customer consent to follow the new confidentiality practice with respect to the customer's confidential information.

System security-related criteria relevant to confidentiality

3.8   Procedures exist to restrict logical access to the system and the confidential information resources maintained in the system including, but not limited to, the following matters:

Criteria

a. Logical access security measures to restrict access to information resources not deemed to be public

b. Identification and authentication of all users.

c. Registration and authorization of new users.

d. The process to make changes and updates to user profiles.

e. Procedures to prevent customers, groups of individuals, or other entities from accessing confidential information other than their own.

f. Procedures to limit access to confidential information to only authorized employees based upon their assigned roles and responsibilities.

g. Distribution of output containing confidential information restricted to authorized users.

h. Restriction of access to offline storage, backup data, systems, and media.

i. Restriction of access to system configurations, superuser functionality, master passwords, powerful utilities, and security devices (for example, firewalls).

3.9 Procedures exist to restrict physical access to the defined system including, but not limited to, facilities, backup media, and other system components such as firewalls, routers, and servers.

3.10 Procedures exist to protect against unauthorized access to system resources.

3.11 Procedures exist to protect against infection by computer viruses, malicious code, and unauthorized software.

3.12 Encryption or other equivalent security techniques are used to protect transmissions of user authentication and other confidential information passed over the Internet or other public networks.

Criteria related to execution and incident management used to achieve the objectives

3.13 Procedures exist to identify, report, and act upon system confidentiality and security breaches and other incidents.

Criteria related to the system components used to achieve the objectives

3.14 Procedures exist to provide that system data are classified in accordance with the defined confidentiality and related security policies.

3.15 Procedures exist to provide that issues of noncompliance with defined confidentiality and related security policies are promptly addressed and that corrective measures are taken on a timely basis.

3.16 Design, acquisition, implementation, configuration, modification, and management of infrastructure and software are consistent with defined confidentiality and related security policies.

(continued)

AAG-SOP APP B

	Criteria
3.17	Procedures exist to help ensure that personnel responsible for the design, development, implementation, and operation of systems affecting confidentiality and security have the qualifications and resources to fulfill their responsibilities.
	Change management-related criteria relevant to confidentiality
3.18	Procedures exist to maintain system components, including configurations consistent with the defined system confidentiality and related security policies.
3.19	Procedures exist to provide that only authorized, tested, and documented changes are made to the system.
3.20	Procedures exist to provide that emergency changes are documented and authorized (including after-the-fact approval).
3.21	Procedures exist to provide that confidential information is protected during the system development, testing, and change processes in accordance with defined system confidentiality and related security policies.
4.0	**Monitoring: The entity monitors the system and takes action to maintain compliance with its defined confidentiality policies.**
4.1	The entity's system confidentiality and security performance is periodically reviewed and compared with the defined system confidentiality and related security policies.
4.2	There is a process to identify and address potential impairments to the entity's ongoing ability to achieve its objectives in accordance with its system confidentiality and related security policies.
4.3	Environmental, regulatory, and technological changes are monitored, and their impact on system confidentiality and security is assessed on a timely basis. System confidentiality policies and procedures are updated for such changes as required.

Generally Accepted Privacy Principles and Criteria

Ref.	*Management Principle and Criteria*
1.0	**The entity defines, documents, communicates, and assigns accountability for its privacy policies and procedures.**
1.1	**Policies and Communications**
1.1.0	**Privacy Policies**
	The entity defines and documents its privacy policies with respect to the following:
	a. Notice (See 2.1.0)
	b. Choice and consent (See 3.1.0)
	c. Collection (See 4.1.0)

Ref.	Management Principle and Criteria
	d. Use, retention, and disposal (See 5.1.0)
	e. Access (See 6.1.0)
	f. Disclosure to third parties (See 7.1.0)
	g. Security for privacy (See 8.1.0)
	h. Quality (See 9.1.0)
	i. Monitoring and enforcement (See 10.1.0)
1.1.1	**Communication to Internal Personnel**
	Privacy policies and the consequences of noncompliance with such policies are communicated, at least annually, to the entity's internal personnel responsible for collecting, using, retaining, and disclosing personal information. Changes in privacy policies are communicated to such personnel shortly after the changes are approved.
1.1.2	**Responsibility and Accountability for Policies**
	Responsibility and accountability are assigned to a person or group for developing, documenting, implementing, enforcing, monitoring, and updating the entity's privacy policies. The names of such person or group and their responsibilities are communicated to internal personnel.
1.2	**Procedures and Controls**
1.2.1	**Review and Approval**
	Privacy policies and procedures, and changes thereto, are reviewed and approved by management.
1.2.2	**Consistency of Privacy Policies and Procedures With Laws and Regulations**
	Policies and procedures are reviewed and compared to the requirements of applicable laws and regulations at least annually and whenever changes to such laws and regulations are made. Privacy policies and procedures are revised to conform with the requirements of applicable laws and regulations.
1.2.3	**Personal Information Identification and Classification**
	The types of personal information and sensitive personal information and the related processes, systems, and third parties involved in the handling of such information are identified. Such information is covered by the entity's privacy and related security policies and procedures.
1.2.4	**Risk Assessment**
	A risk assessment process is used to establish a risk baseline and to, at least annually, identify new or changed risks to personal information and to develop and update responses to such risks.
1.2.5	**Consistency of Commitments With Privacy Policies and Procedures**
	Internal personnel or advisers review contracts for consistency with privacy policies and procedures and address any inconsistencies.

(continued)

Ref.	Management Principle and Criteria
1.2.6	**Infrastructure and Systems Management**

The potential privacy impact is assessed when new processes involving personal information are implemented, and when changes are made to such processes (including any such activities outsourced to third parties or contractors), and personal information continues to be protected in accordance with the privacy policies. For this purpose, processes involving personal information include the design, acquisition, development, implementation, configuration, modification and management of the following:

- Infrastructure
- Systems
- Applications
- Websites
- Procedures
- Products and services
- Data bases and information repositories
- Mobile computing and other similar electronic devices

The use of personal information in process and system test and development is prohibited unless such information is anonymized or otherwise protected in accordance with the entity's privacy policies and procedures.

| 1.2.7 | **Privacy Incident and Breach Management** |

A documented privacy incident and breach management program has been implemented that includes, but is not limited to, the following:

- Procedures for the identification, management, and resolution of privacy incidents and breaches
- Defined responsibilities
- A process to identify incident severity and determine required actions and escalation procedures
- A process for complying with breach laws and regulations, including stakeholders breach notification, if required
- An accountability process for employees or third parties responsible for incidents or breaches with remediation, penalties, or discipline as appropriate
- A process for periodic review (at least on an annual basis) of actual incidents to identify necessary program updates based on the following:
  - Incident patterns and root cause
  - Changes in the internal control environment or external requirements (regulation or legislation)
- Periodic testing or walkthrough process (at least on an annual basis) and associated program remediation as needed

Ref.	*Management Principle and Criteria*
1.2.8	**Supporting Resources** Resources are provided by the entity to implement and support its privacy policies.
1.2.9	**Qualifications of Internal Personnel** The entity establishes qualifications for personnel responsible for protecting the privacy and security of personal information and assigns such responsibilities only to those personnel who meet these qualifications and have received needed training.
1.2.10	**Privacy Awareness and Training** A privacy awareness program about the entity's privacy policies and related matters, and specific training for selected personnel depending on their roles and responsibilities, are provided.
1.2.11	**Changes in Regulatory and Business Requirements** For each jurisdiction in which the entity operates, the effect on privacy requirements from changes in the following factors is identified and addressed: • Legal and regulatory • Contracts, including service-level agreements • Industry requirements • Business operations and processes • People, roles, and responsibilities • Technology Privacy policies and procedures are updated to reflect changes in requirements.

Notice

Ref.	*Notice Principle and Criteria*
2.0	**The entity provides notice about its privacy policies and procedures and identifies the purposes for which personal information is collected, used, retained, and disclosed.**
2.1	**Policies and Communications**
2.1.0	**Privacy Policies** The entity's privacy policies address providing notice to individuals.
2.1.1	**Communication to Individuals** Notice is provided to individuals regarding the following privacy policies: *a.* Purpose for collecting personal information *b.* Choice and consent (See 3.1.1) *c.* Collection (See 4.1.1)

(continued)

Ref.	Notice Principle and Criteria
	d. Use, retention, and disposal (See 5.1.1)
	e. Access (See 6.1.1)
	f. Disclosure to third parties (See 7.1.1)
	g. Security for privacy (See 8.1.1)
	h. Quality (See 9.1.1)
	i. Monitoring and enforcement (See 10.1.1)
	If personal information is collected from sources other than the individual, such sources are described in the notice.
2.2	**Procedures and Controls**
2.2.1	**Provision of Notice**
	Notice is provided to the individual about the entity's privacy policies and procedures (a) at or before the time personal information is collected, or as soon as practical thereafter, (b) at or before the entity changes its privacy policies and procedures, or as soon as practical thereafter, or (c) before personal information is used for new purposes not previously identified.
2.2.2	**Entities and Activities Covered**
	An objective description of the entities and activities covered by the privacy policies and procedures is included in the entity's privacy notice.
2.2.3	**Clear and Conspicuous**
	The entity's privacy notice is conspicuous and uses clear language.

Choice and Consent

Ref.	Choice and Consent Principle and Criteria
3.0	**The entity describes the choices available to the individual and obtains implicit or explicit consent with respect to the collection, use, and disclosure of personal information.**
3.1	**Policies and Communications**
3.1.0	**Privacy Policies**
	The entity's privacy policies address the choices available to individuals and the consent to be obtained.
3.1.1	**Communication to Individuals**
	Individuals are informed about (a) the choices available to them with respect to the collection, use, and disclosure of personal information, and (b) that implicit or explicit consent is required to collect, use, and disclose personal information, unless a law or regulation specifically requires or allows otherwise.

Ref.	Choice and Consent Principle and Criteria
3.1.2	**Consequences of Denying or Withdrawing Consent**
	When personal information is collected, individuals are informed of the consequences of refusing to provide personal information or of denying or withdrawing consent to use personal information for purposes identified in the notice.
3.2	**Procedures and Controls**
3.2.1	**Implicit or Explicit Consent**
	Implicit or explicit consent is obtained from the individual at or before the time personal information is collected or soon after. The individual's preferences expressed in his or her consent are confirmed and implemented.
3.2.2	**Consent for New Purposes and Uses**
	If information that was previously collected is to be used for purposes not previously identified in the privacy notice, the new purpose is documented, the individual is notified, and implicit or explicit consent is obtained prior to such new use or purpose.
3.2.3	**Explicit Consent for Sensitive Information**
	Explicit consent is obtained directly from the individual when sensitive personal information is collected, used, or disclosed, unless a law or regulation specifically requires otherwise.
3.2.4	**Consent for Online Data Transfers To or From an Individual's Computer or Other Similar Electronic Devices**
	Consent is obtained before personal information is transferred to or from an individual's computer or other similar device.

Collection

Ref.	Collection Principle and Criteria
4.0	**The entity collects personal information only for the purposes identified in the notice.**
4.1	**Policies and Communications**
4.1.0	**Privacy Policies**
	The entity's privacy policies address the collection of personal information.
4.1.1	**Communication to Individuals**
	Individuals are informed that personal information is collected only for the purposes identified in the notice.
4.1.2	**Types of Personal Information Collected and Methods of Collection**
	The types of personal information collected and the methods of collection, including the use of cookies or other tracking techniques, are documented and described in the privacy notice.

(continued)

Ref.	Collection Principle and Criteria
4.2	**Procedures and Controls**
4.2.1	**Collection Limited to Identified Purpose**
	The collection of personal information is limited to that necessary for the purposes identified in the notice.
4.2.2	**Collection by Fair and Lawful Means**
	Methods of collecting personal information are reviewed by management before they are implemented to confirm that personal information is obtained (*a*) fairly, without intimidation or deception, and (*b*) lawfully, adhering to all relevant rules of law, whether derived from statute or common law, relating to the collection of personal information.
4.2.3	**Collection From Third Parties**
	Management confirms that third parties from whom personal information is collected (that is, sources other than the individual) are reliable sources that collect information fairly and lawfully
4.2.4	**Information Developed about Individuals**
	Individuals are informed if the entity develops or acquires additional information about them for its use.

Use, Retention, and Disposal

Ref.	Use, Retention, and Disposal Principle and Criteria
5.0	**The entity limits the use of personal information to the purposes identified in the notice and for which the individual has provided implicit or explicit consent. The entity retains personal information for only as long as necessary to fulfill the stated purposes or as required by law or regulations and thereafter appropriately disposes of such information.**
5.1	**Policies and Communications**
5.1.0	**Privacy Policies**
	The entity's privacy policies address the use, retention, and disposal of personal information.
5.1.1	**Communication to Individuals**
	Individuals are informed that personal information is (*a*) used only for the purposes identified in the notice and only if the individual has provided implicit or explicit consent, unless a law or regulation specifically requires otherwise, (*b*) retained for no longer than necessary to fulfill the stated purposes, or for a period specifically required by law or regulation, and (*c*) disposed of in a manner that prevents loss, theft, misuse, or unauthorized access.

Ref.	Use, Retention, and Disposal Principle and Criteria
5.2	**Procedures and Controls**
5.2.1	**Use of Personal Information**
	Personal information is used only for the purposes identified in the notice and only if the individual has provided implicit or explicit consent, unless a law or regulation specifically requires otherwise.
5.2.2	**Retention of Personal Information**
	Personal information is retained for no longer than necessary to fulfill the stated purposes unless a law or regulation specifically requires otherwise.
5.2.3	**Disposal, Destruction and Redaction of Personal Information**
	Personal information no longer retained is anonymized, disposed of, or destroyed in a manner that prevents loss, theft, misuse, or unauthorized access.

Access

Ref.	Access Principle and Criteria
6.0	**The entity provides individuals with access to their personal information for review and update.**
6.1	**Policies and Communications**
6.1.0	**Privacy Policies**
	The entity's privacy policies address providing individuals with access to their personal information.
6.1.1	**Communication to Individuals**
	Individuals are informed about how they may obtain access to their personal information to review, update, and correct that information.
6.2	**Procedures and Controls**
6.2.1	**Access by Individuals to Their Personal Information**
	Individuals are able to determine whether the entity maintains personal information about them and, upon request, may obtain access to their personal information.
6.2.2	**Confirmation of an Individual's Identity**
	The identity of individuals who request access to their personal information is authenticated before they are given access to that information.
6.2.3	**Understandable Personal Information, Time Frame, and Cost**
	Personal information is provided to the individual in an understandable form, in a reasonable timeframe, and at a reasonable cost, if any.

(continued)

Ref.	Access Principle and Criteria
6.2.4	**Denial of Access**
	Individuals are informed, in writing, of the reason a request for access to their personal information was denied, the source of the entity's legal right to deny such access, if applicable, and the individual's right, if any, to challenge such denial, as specifically permitted or required by law or regulation.
6.2.5	**Updating or Correcting Personal Information**
	Individuals are able to update or correct personal information held by the entity. If practical and economically feasible to do so, the entity provides such updated or corrected information to third parties that previously were provided with the individual's personal information.
6.2.6	**Statement of Disagreement**
	Individuals are informed, in writing, about the reason a request for correction of personal information was denied, and how they may appeal.

Disclosure to Third Parties

Ref.	Disclosure to Third Parties Principle and Criteria
7.0	**The entity discloses personal information to third parties only for the purposes identified in the notice and with the implicit or explicit consent of the individual.**
7.1	**Policies and Communications**
7.1.0	**Privacy Policies**
	The entity's privacy policies address the disclosure of personal information to third parties.
7.1.1	**Communication to Individuals**
	Individuals are informed that personal information is disclosed to third parties only for the purposes identified in the notice and for which the individual has provided implicit or explicit consent unless a law or regulation specifically allows or requires otherwise.
7.1.2	**Communication to Third Parties**
	Privacy policies or other specific instructions or requirements for handling personal information are communicated to third parties to whom personal information is disclosed.
7.2	**Procedures and Controls**
7.2.1	**Disclosure of Personal Information**
	Personal information is disclosed to third parties only for the purposes described in the notice, and for which the individual has provided implicit or explicit consent, unless a law or regulation specifically requires or allows otherwise.

Ref.	Disclosure to Third Parties Principle and Criteria
7.2.2	**Protection of Personal Information** Personal information is disclosed only to third parties who have agreements with the entity to protect personal information in a manner consistent with the relevant aspects of the entity's privacy policies or other specific instructions or requirements. The entity has procedures in place to evaluate that the third parties have effective controls to meet the terms of the agreement, instructions, or requirements.
7.2.3	**New Purposes and Uses** Personal information is disclosed to third parties for new purposes or uses only with the prior implicit or explicit consent of the individual.
7.2.4	**Misuse of Personal Information by a Third Party** The entity takes remedial action in response to misuse of personal information by a third party to whom the entity has transferred such information.

Security for Privacy

Ref.	Security for Privacy Principle and Criteria
8.0	**The entity protects personal information against unauthorized access (both physical and logical).**
8.1	**Policies and Communications**
8.1.0	**Privacy Policies** The entity's privacy policies (including any relevant security policies), address the security of personal information.
8.1.1	**Communication to Individuals** Individuals are informed that precautions are taken to protect personal information.
8.2	**Procedures and Controls**
8.2.1	**Information Security Program** A security program has been developed, documented, approved, and implemented that includes administrative, technical, and physical safeguards to protect personal information from loss, misuse, unauthorized access, disclosure, alteration, and destruction. The security program should address, but not be limited to, the following areas[1] insofar as they relate to the security of personal information:

(continued)

---

[1] These areas are drawn from ISO/IEC 27002:2005, Information technology—Security techniques—Code of practice for information security management. Permission is granted by the American National Standards Institute (ANSI) on behalf of the International Organization for Standardization (ISO). Copies of ISO/IEC 27002 can be purchased from ANSI in the United States at http://webstore.ansi.org/ and in Canada from the Standards Council of Canada at www.standardsstore .ca/eSpecs/index.jsp. It is not necessary to meet all of the criteria of ISO/IEC 27002:2005 to satisfy *Generally Accepted Privacy Principles'* criterion 8.2.1. The references associated with each area indicate the most relevant *Generally Accepted Privacy Principles'* criteria for this purpose.

Ref.	Security for Privacy Principle and Criteria
	a. Risk assessment and treatment [1.2.4]
	b. Security policy [8.1.0]
	c. Organization of information security [sections 1, 7, and 10]
	d. Asset management [section 1]
	e. Human resources security [section 1]
	f. Physical and environmental security [8.2.3 and 8.2.4]
	g. Communications and operations management [sections 1, 7, and 10]
	h. Access control [sections 1, 8.2, and 10]
	i. Information systems acquisition, development, and maintenance [1.2.6]
	j. Information security incident management [1.2.7]
	k. Business continuity management [section 8.2]
	l. Compliance [sections 1 and 10]
8.2.2	**Logical Access Controls**
	Logical access to personal information is restricted by procedures that address the following matters:
	a. Authorizing and registering internal personnel and individuals
	b. Identifying and authenticating internal personnel and individuals
	c. Making changes and updating access profiles
	d. Granting privileges and permissions for access to IT infrastructure components and personal information
	e. Preventing individuals from accessing anything other than their own personal or sensitive information
	f. Limiting access to personal information to only authorized internal personnel based upon their assigned roles and responsibilities
	g. Distributing output only to authorized internal personnel
	h. Restricting logical access to offline storage, backup data, systems, and media
	i. Restricting access to system configurations, superuser functionality, master passwords, powerful utilities, and security devices (for example, firewalls)
	j. Preventing the introduction of viruses, malicious code, and unauthorized software
8.2.3	**Physical Access Controls**
	Physical access is restricted to personal information in any form (including the components of the entity's system(s) that contain or protect personal information).
8.2.4	**Environmental Safeguards**
	Personal information, in all forms, is protected against accidental disclosure due to natural disasters and environmental hazards.

Ref.	Security for Privacy Principle and Criteria
8.2.5	**Transmitted Personal Information**
	Personal information is protected when transmitted by mail or other physical means. Personal information collected and transmitted over the Internet, over public and other nonsecure networks, and wireless networks is protected by deploying industry standard encryption technology for transferring and receiving personal information.
8.2.6	**Personal Information on Portable Media**
	Personal information stored on portable media or devices is protected from unauthorized access.
8.2.7	**Testing Security Safeguards**
	Tests of the effectiveness of the key administrative, technical, and physical safeguards protecting personal information are conducted at least annually.

Quality

Ref.	Quality Principle and Criteria
9.0	**The entity maintains accurate, complete, and relevant personal information for the purposes identified in the notice.**
9.1	**Policies and Communications**
9.1.0	**Privacy Policies**
	The entity's privacy policies address the quality of personal information.
9.1.1	**Communication to Individuals**
	Individuals are informed that they are responsible for providing the entity with accurate and complete personal information, and for contacting the entity if correction of such information is required.
9.2	**Procedures and Controls**
9.2.1	**Accuracy and Completeness of Personal Information**
	Personal information is accurate and complete for the purposes for which it is to be used.
9.2.2	**Relevance of Personal Information**
	Personal information is relevant to the purposes for which it is to be used.

Monitoring and Enforcement

Ref.	Monitoring and Enforcement Principle and Criteria
10.0	**The entity monitors compliance with its privacy policies and procedures and has procedures to address privacy related inquiries, complaints and disputes.**
10.1	**Policies and Communications**
10.1.0	**Privacy Policies** The entity's privacy policies address the monitoring and enforcement of privacy policies and procedures.
10.1.1	**Communication to Individuals** Individuals are informed about how to contact the entity with inquiries, complaints and disputes.
10.2	**Procedures and Controls**
10.2.1	**Inquiry, Complaint, and Dispute Process** A process is in place to address inquiries, complaints, and disputes.
10.2.2	**Dispute Resolution and Recourse** Each complaint is addressed, and the resolution is documented and communicated to the individual.
10.2.3	**Compliance Review** Compliance with privacy policies and procedures, commitments and applicable laws, regulations, service-level agreements, and other contracts is reviewed and documented, and the results of such reviews are reported to management. If problems are identified, remediation plans are developed and implemented.
10.2.4	**Instances of Noncompliance** Instances of noncompliance with privacy policies and procedures are documented and reported and, if needed, corrective and disciplinary measures are taken on a timely basis.
10.2.5	**Ongoing Monitoring** Ongoing procedures are performed for monitoring the effectiveness of controls over personal information, based on a risk assessment [1.2.4], and for taking timely corrective actions where necessary.

Appendix C

Illustrative Management Assertions and Related Service Auditor's Reports on Controls at a Service Organization Relevant to Security, Availability, Processing Integrity, Confidentiality, and Privacy

This appendix presents two examples of management's assertion, each followed by the related service auditor's report. The following table summarizes how these examples differ:

	Example 1	*Example 2*
Principles covered by management's assertion and the service auditor's report	Security, availability, processing integrity, and confidentiality.	Privacy.
Need for complementary user-entity controls at the user entities	Complementary user-entity controls are needed to meet certain applicable trust services criteria. Modifications to the report are shown in boldface italics.	Complementary user-entity controls are not needed to meet certain applicable trust services criteria.
Placement of the description criteria in management's assertion	The description criteria are presented immediately after management's assertion about the fairness of the presentation of the description of the service organization's system.	The description criteria are presented after all of management's assertions.

Example 1: Illustrative Management Assertion on Controls at a Service Organization Relevant to the Security, Availability, Processing Integrity, and Confidentiality Principles

Management of XYZ Service Organization's Assertion
Regarding Its Accurate
Claims Processing System for the Period January 1, 20X1, to
December 31, 20X1

We have prepared the attached description titled "Description of XYZ Service Organization's Accurate Claims Processing System for the Period January 1, 20X1, to December 31, 20X1" (the description), based on the criteria in items (a)(i)–(ii) below, which are the criteria for a description of a service organization's system in paragraphs 1.33–.34 of the AICPA Guide *Reporting on Controls at a Service Organization Relevant to Security, Availability, Processing Integrity, Confidentiality, or Privacy* (the description criteria). The description is intended to provide users with information about the Accurate Claims Processing System, particularly system controls intended to meet the criteria for the security, availability, processing integrity, and confidentiality principles set forth in TSP section 100, *Trust Services Principles, Criteria, and Illustrations for Security, Availability, Processing Integrity, Confidentiality, and Privacy* (AICPA, *Technical Practice Aids*) (applicable trust services criteria). We confirm, to the best of our knowledge and belief, that

　　a. the description fairly presents the [*type or name of*] system throughout the period [*date*] to [*date*], based on the following description criteria:

　　　　i. The description contains the following information:

　　　　　　(1) The types of services provided

　　　　　　(2) The components of the system used to provide the services, which are the following:

　　　　　　　　● *Infrastructure.* The physical and hardware components of a system (facilities, equipment, and networks).

　　　　　　　　● *Software.* The programs and operating software of a system (systems, applications, and utilities).

　　　　　　　　● *People.* The personnel involved in the operation and use of a system (developers, operators, users, and managers).

　　　　　　　　● *Procedures.* The automated and manual procedures involved in the operation of a system.

　　　　　　　　● *Data.* The information used and supported by a system (transaction streams, files, databases, and tables).

　　　　　　(3) The boundaries or aspects of the system covered by the description

(4) How the system captures and addresses significant events and conditions

(5) The process used to prepare and deliver reports and other information to user entities and other parties

(6) If information is provided to, or received from, subservice organizations or other parties, how such information is provided or received; the role of the subservice organization and other parties; and the procedures performed to determine that such information and its processing, maintenance, and storage are subject to appropriate controls

(7) For each principle being reported on, the applicable trust services criteria and the related controls designed to meet those criteria, including, as applicable, complementary user-entity controls contemplated in the design of the service organization's system

(8) For subservice organizations presented using the carve-out method, the nature of the services provided by the subservice organization; each of the applicable trust services criteria that are intended to be met by controls at the subservice organization, alone or in combination with controls at the service organization, and the types of controls expected to be implemented at carved-out subservice organizations to meet those criteria; and for privacy, the types of activities that the subservice organization would need to perform to comply with our privacy commitments

(9) Any applicable trust services criteria that are not addressed by a control at the service organization or a subservice organization and the reasons therefore

(10) Other aspects of the service organization's control environment, risk assessment process, information and communication systems, and monitoring of controls that are relevant to the services provided and the applicable trust services criteria

(11) Relevant details of changes to the service organization's system during the period covered by the description

ii. The description does not omit or distort information relevant to the service organization's system while acknowledging that the description is prepared to meet the common needs of a broad range of users and may not, therefore, include every aspect of the system that each individual user may consider important to his or her own particular needs.

  b. the controls stated in description were suitably designed throughout the specified period to meet the applicable trust services criteria.

  c. the controls stated in the description operated effectively throughout the specified period to meet the applicable trust services criteria.

Example 1: Illustrative Service Auditor's Report on Controls at a Service Organization Relevant to Security, Availability, Processing Integrity, and Confidentiality

(Language shown in boldface italics represents modifications that would be made to the service auditor's report if complementary user-entity controls are needed to meet certain applicable trust services criteria.)

Independent Service Auditor's Report

To: XYZ Service Organization

Scope

We have examined the attached description titled "Description of XYZ Service Organization's Accurate Claims Processing System for the Period January 1, 20X1, to December 31, 20X1"[1] (the description) and the suitability of the design and operating effectiveness of controls to meet the criteria for the security, availability, processing integrity, and confidentiality principles set forth in TSP section 100, *Trust Services Principles, Criteria, and Illustrations for Security, Availability, Processing Integrity, Confidentiality, and Privacy* (AICPA, *Technical Practice Aids*) (applicable trust services criteria), throughout the period January 1, 20X1, to December 31, 20X1. ***The description indicates that certain applicable trust services criteria specified in the description can be achieved only if complementary user-entity controls contemplated in the design of XYZ Service Organization's controls are suitably designed and operating effectively, along with related controls at the service organization. We have not evaluated the suitability of the design or operating effectiveness of such complementary user-entity controls.***

Service organization's responsibilities

XYZ Service Organization has provided the attached assertion titled "Management of XYZ Service Organization's Assertion Regarding Its Accurate Claims Processing System for the Period January 1, 20X1, to December 31, 20X1,"[2] which is based on the criteria identified in management's assertion. XYZ Service Organization is responsible for (1) preparing the description and assertion; (2) the completeness, accuracy, and method of presentation of both the description and assertion; (3) providing the services covered by the description; (4) specifying the controls that meet the applicable trust services criteria and stating them in the description; and (5) designing, implementing, and documenting the controls to meet the applicable trust services criteria.

Service auditor's responsibilities

Our responsibility is to express an opinion on the fairness of the presentation of the description based on the description criteria set forth in XYZ Service Organization's assertion and on the suitability of the design and operating effectiveness of the controls to meet the applicable trust services criteria, based on our examination. We conducted our examination in accordance with attestation standards established by the American Institute of Certified Public

---

[1] The title of the description of the service organization's system in the service auditor's report should be the same as the title used by management of the service organization in its description of the service organization's system.

[2] The title of the assertion in the service auditor's report should be the same as the title used by management of the service organization in its assertion.

Accountants. Those standards require that we plan and perform our examination to obtain reasonable assurance about whether, in all material respects, (1) the description is fairly presented based on the description criteria, and (2) the controls were suitably designed and operating effectively to meet the applicable trust services criteria throughout the period January 1, 20X1, to December 31, 20X1.

Our examination involved performing procedures to obtain evidence about the fairness of the presentation of the description based on the description criteria and the suitability of the design and operating effectiveness of those controls to meet the applicable trust services criteria. Our procedures included assessing the risks that the description is not fairly presented and that the controls were not suitably designed or operating effectively to meet the applicable trust services criteria. Our procedures also included testing the operating effectiveness of those controls that we consider necessary to provide reasonable assurance that the applicable trust services criteria were met. Our examination also included evaluating the overall presentation of the description. We believe that the evidence we obtained is sufficient and appropriate to provide a reasonable basis for our opinion.

Inherent limitations

Because of their nature and inherent limitations, controls at a service organization may not always operate effectively to meet the applicable trust services criteria. Also, the projection to the future of any evaluation of the fairness of the presentation of the description or conclusions about the suitability of the design or operating effectiveness of the controls to meet the applicable trust services criteria is subject to the risks that the system may change or that controls at a service organization may become inadequate or fail.

Opinion

In our opinion, in all material respects, based on the description criteria identified in XYZ Service Organization's assertion and the applicable trust services criteria

a. the description fairly presents the system that was designed and implemented throughout the period January 1, 20X1, to December 31, 20X1.

b. the controls stated in the description were suitably designed to provide reasonable assurance that the applicable trust services criteria would be met if the controls operated effectively throughout the period January 1, 20X1 to December 31, 20X1, *and user entities applied the complementary user-entity controls contemplated in the design of XYZ Service Organization's controls throughout the period January 1, 20X1, to December 31, 20X1*.

c. the controls tested, which *together with the complementary user-entity controls referred to in the scope paragraph of this report, if operating effectively,* were those necessary to provide reasonable assurance that the applicable trust services criteria were met, operated effectively throughout the period January 1, 20X1, to December 31, 20X1.

Description of tests of controls

The specific controls we tested and the nature, timing, and results of our tests are presented in the section of our report titled "Description of Test of Controls and Results Thereof."

AAG-SOP APP C

Intended use

This report and the description of tests of controls and results thereof are intended solely for the information and use of XYZ Service Organization; user entities of XYZ Service Organization's Accurate Claims Processing System during some or all of the period January 1, 20X1, to December 31, 20X1; and prospective user entities, independent auditors and practitioners providing services to such user entities, and regulators who have sufficient knowledge and understanding of the following:

- The nature of the service provided by the service organization
- How the service organization's system interacts with user entities, subservice organizations, and other parties
- Internal control and its limitations
- Complementary user-entity controls and how they interact with related controls at the service organization to meet the applicable trust services criteria
- The applicable trust services criteria
- The risks that may threaten the achievement of the applicable trust services criteria and how controls address those risks

This report is not intended to be and should not be used by anyone other than these specified parties.

[Service auditor's signature]

[Date of the service auditor's report]

[Service auditor's city and state]

Example 2: Illustrative Management Assertion Regarding a Description of a Service Organization's System, the Suitability of the Design and Operating Effectiveness of Its Controls Relevant to the Privacy Principle, and Its Compliance With Commitments in Its Statement of Privacy Practices

Management of XYZ Service Organization's Assertion

We have prepared the attached description titled [*title of the description*][3] (the description) of XYZ Service Organization's [*type or name of*] system and our statement of privacy practices[4] related to XYZ Service Organization's [*type or name of*] service. The description is intended to provide users with information about our system, particularly system controls intended to meet the criteria for the privacy principle set forth in TSP section 100, *Trust Services Principles, Criteria, and Illustrations for Security, Availability, Processing Integrity, Confidentiality, and Privacy* (AICPA, *Technical Practice Aids*)[5] (applicable trust services criteria). We confirm, to the best of our knowledge and belief, that

- the description fairly presents the [*type or name of*] system throughout the period [*date*] to [*date*]. The criteria for the description are identified below under the heading "Description Criteria."

- the controls stated in the description were suitably designed and operated effectively throughout the period [*date*] to [*date*] to meet the criteria for the privacy principle set forth in TSP section 100 (the applicable trust services criteria).

- we complied with the commitments in our statement of privacy practices, in all material respects, throughout the period [*date*] to [*date*].

Description Criteria

In preparing our description and making our assertion regarding the fairness of the presentation of the description, we used the criteria in items (a)–(b) below, which are the criteria in paragraphs 1.33–.34 of the AICPA Guide *Reporting on Controls at a Service Organization Relevant to Security, Availability, Processing Integrity, Confidentiality, or Privacy*:

    a. The description contains the following information:

        i. The types of services provided.

---

[3] Insert the title of the description of the service organization's system used by management of the service organization in its description (for example, "Description of XYZ Service Organization's Claims-Processing System Throughout the Period January 1, 20X1, to December 31, 20X1, Including its Statement of Privacy Practices").

[4] In many cases, the user entities provide a privacy notice to the individuals about whom information is collected. In such cases, the service organization would prepare a statement of privacy practices for use by the user entities to describe its practices and commitments to user entities related to the matters typically included in a privacy notice to individuals. If the service organization is responsible for providing the privacy notice directly to individuals, such notice may be a suitable substitute for a statement of privacy practices.

[5] The criteria for privacy are also set forth in *Generally Accepted Privacy Principles* issued by the AICPA and the Canadian Institute of Chartered Accountants, which could be referenced here instead of TSP section 100, *Trust Services Principles, Criteria, and Illustrations for Security, Availability, Processing Integrity, Confidentiality, and Privacy* (AICPA, *Technical Practice Aids*).

ii. The components of the system used to provide the services, which are the following:

(1) *Infrastructure*. The physical and hardware components of a system (facilities, equipment, and networks).

(2) *Software*. The programs and operating software of a system (systems, applications, and utilities).

(3) *People*. The personnel involved in the operation and use of a system (developers, operators, users, and managers).

(4) *Procedures*. The automated and manual procedures involved in the operation of a system.

(5) *Data*. The information used and supported by a system (transaction streams, files, databases, and tables).

iii. The boundaries or aspects of the system covered by the description and the service auditor's report. As it relates to the privacy of information, a system includes, at a minimum, all system components directly or indirectly related to the collection, use, retention, disclosure, and disposal or anonymization of personal information throughout its personal information life cycle.

iv. The types of personal information collected from individuals or obtained from user entities or other parties and how such information is collected and, if collected by user entities, how it is obtained by the service organization.

v. The process for (1) identifying specific requirements in agreements with user entities and laws and regulations applicable to personal information and (2) implementing controls and practices to meet those requirements.

vi. If the service organization provides the privacy notice to individuals about whom personal information is collected, used, retained, disclosed, and disposed of or anonymized, the privacy notice prepared in conformity with the relevant criteria for a privacy notice set forth in TSP section 100.

vii. If the user entities, rather than the service organization, are responsible for providing the privacy notice to individuals, a statement regarding how the privacy notice is communicated to individuals, that the user entities are responsible for communicating such notice to the individuals, and that the service organization is responsible for communicating its privacy practices to the user entities in its statement of privacy practices, which includes the following information:

(1) A summary of the significant privacy and related security requirements common to most agreements between the service organization and its user entities and any requirements in a user-entity agreement that the service organization meets for all or most user entities

(2) A summary of the significant privacy and related security requirements mandated by law, regulation, an industry, or a market that the service organization meets for all or most user entities that are not included in user-entity agreements

(3) The purposes, uses, and disclosures of personal information as permitted by user-entity agreements and beyond those permitted by such agreements but not prohibited by such agreements and the service organization's commitments regarding the purpose, use, and disclosure of personal information that are prohibited by such agreements

(4) A statement that the information will be retained for a period no longer than necessary to fulfill the stated purposes or contractual requirements or for the period required by law or regulation, as applicable, or a statement describing other retention practices

(5) A statement that the information will be disposed of in a manner that prevents loss, theft, misuse, or unauthorized access to the information

(6) If applicable, how the service organization supports any process permitted by user entities for individuals to obtain access to their information to review, update, or correct it

(7) If applicable, a description of the process to determine that personal information is accurate and complete and how the service organization implements correction processes permitted by user entities

(8) If applicable, how inquiries, complaints, and disputes from individuals (whether directly from the individual or indirectly through user entities) regarding their personal information are handled by the service organization

(9) A statement regarding the existence of a written security program and what industry or other standards it is based on

(10) Other relevant information related to privacy practices deemed appropriate for user entities by the service organization

viii. If the user entities, rather than the service organization, are responsible for providing the privacy notice to individuals, the service organization's statement of privacy practices.

ix. How the system captures and addresses significant events and conditions.

x. The process used to deliver services, reports, and other information to user entities and other parties.

    xi. If information is provided to, or received from, subservice organizations or third parties

        (1) how such information is provided or received and the role of the subservice organizations or other parties.

        (2) the procedures performed to determine that such information is protected in conformity with the service organization's statement of privacy practices.

    xii. For each principle being reported on, the applicable trust services criteria and the related controls designed to meet those criteria, including, as applicable, complementary user-entity controls contemplated in the design of the service organization's system.

    xiii. For subservice organizations presented using the carve-out method

        (1) the nature of the services provided by the subservice organization.

        (2) if the description addresses the privacy principle, any aspects of the personal information life cycle for which responsibility has been delegated to the subservice organization, if applicable.

        (3) each of the applicable trust services criteria that are intended to be met by controls at the subservice organization, alone or in combination with controls at the service organization, and the types of controls expected to be implemented at carved-out subservice organizations to meet those criteria.

        (4) if the description addresses the privacy principle, the types of activities that the subservice organization would need to perform to comply with the service organization's privacy commitments.

    xiv. Any applicable trust services criteria that are not addressed by a control at the service organization or subservice organization and the reasons therefore.

    xv. Other aspects of the service organization's control environment, risk assessment process, information and communication systems, and monitoring of controls that are relevant to the services provided, the personal information life cycle, and the applicable trust services criteria.

    xvi. Relevant details of changes to the service organization's system during the period covered by the description.

b. The description does not omit or distort information relevant to the service organization's system and personal information life cycle while acknowledging that the description is presented to meet the common needs of a broad range of users and may not, therefore, include every aspect of the system and personal information life cycle that each individual user may consider important to his or her own particular needs.

Example 2: Illustrative Service Auditor's Report on a Description of a Service Organization's System, the Suitability of the Design and Operating Effectiveness of Its Controls Relevant to the Privacy Principle, and Its Compliance With Commitments in Its Statement of Privacy Practices

Independent Service Auditor's Report

To: XYZ Service Organization

Scope

We have examined (1) the accompanying description titled [*title of the description*];[6] (2) the suitability of the design and operating effectiveness of controls to meet the criteria for the privacy principle set forth in TSP section 100, *Trust Services Principles, Criteria, and Illustrations for Security, Availability, Processing Integrity, Confidentiality, and Privacy* (AICPA, *Technical Practice Aids*) (applicable trust services criteria); and (3) XYZ Service Organization's compliance with the commitments in its statement of privacy practices throughout the period January 1, 20X1, to December 31, 20X1.

Service organization's responsibilities

XYZ Service Organization has provided the accompanying assertion titled [*title of assertion*].[7] XYZ Service Organization is responsible for (1) preparing the description and assertion; (2) the completeness, accuracy, and method of presentation of both the description and assertion; (3) providing the services covered by the description; (4) specifying the controls that meet the applicable trust services criteria and stating them in the description; (5) designing, implementing, maintaining, and documenting controls to meet the applicable trust services criteria; and (6) complying with the commitments in its statement of privacy practices that is included in the description.

Service auditor's responsibilities

Our responsibility is to express an opinion on (1) the fairness of the presentation of the description based on the description criteria identified in management's assertion; (2) the suitability of the design and operating effectiveness of the controls to meet the applicable trust services criteria; and (3) XYZ Service Organization's compliance with the commitments in its statement of privacy practices, based on our examination. We conducted our examination in accordance with attestation standards established by the American Institute of Certified Public Accountants. Those standards require that we plan and perform our examination to obtain reasonable assurance about whether, in all material respects, (1) the description is fairly presented based on the description criteria, (2) the controls were suitably designed and operating effectively to meet the applicable trust services criteria throughout the period from [*date*] to [*date*], and (3)

---

[6] Insert the title of the description used by management of the service organization (for example, "Description of XYZ Service Organization's Claims Processing System Throughout the Period January 1, 20X1, to December 31, 20X1, Including Its Statement of Privacy Practices").

[7] Insert the title of the assertion used by management of the service organization (for example, "Management of XYZ Service Organization's Assertion Regarding Its Description of the Claims-Processing System, the Suitability of the Design and Operating Effectiveness of Controls, and Compliance With the Commitments in Its Statement of Privacy Practices Throughout the Period January 1, 20X1, to December 31, 20X1").

XYZ Service Organization complied with the commitments in its statement of privacy practices throughout the period from [date] to [date].

Our examination involved performing procedures to obtain evidence about the fairness of the presentation of the description based on the description criteria, the suitability of the design and operating effectiveness of the controls to meet the applicable trust services criteria, and XYZ Service Organization's compliance with the commitments in its statement of privacy practices. Our procedures included assessing the risks that the description is not fairly presented, that the controls were not suitably designed or operating effectively to meet the applicable trust services criteria, and that XYZ Service Organization did not comply with the commitments in its statement of privacy practices. Our procedures also included testing the operating effectiveness of those controls that we consider necessary to provide reasonable assurance that the applicable trust services criteria were met and testing XYZ Service Organization's compliance with the commitments in its statement of privacy practices. Our examination also included evaluating the overall presentation of the description. We believe that the evidence we obtained is sufficient and appropriate to provide a reasonable basis for our opinion.

Inherent limitations

Because of their nature and inherent limitations, controls at a service organization may not always protect personal information against unauthorized access or use nor do they ensure compliance with applicable laws and regulations. For example, fraud or unauthorized access to personal information or unauthorized use or disclosure of personal information by persons authorized to access it may not be prevented or detected, or service organization personnel may not always comply with the commitments in the statement of privacy practices. Also, the projection of any conclusions, based on our findings, to future periods is subject to the risk that any changes or future events may alter the validity of such conclusions.

Opinion

In our opinion, in all material respects, based on the description criteria identified in XYZ Service Organization's assertion and the applicable trust services criteria

    a. the description fairly presents XYZ Service Organization's [*type or name of*] system and related privacy practices that were designed and implemented throughout the period [date] to [date].

    b. the controls stated in the description were suitably designed to provide reasonable assurance that the applicable trust services criteria would be met if the controls operated effectively throughout the period [date] to [date].

    c. the controls we tested, which were those necessary to provide reasonable assurance that the applicable trust services criteria were met, operated effectively throughout the period [date] to [date].

    d. XYZ Service Organization complied with the commitments in its statement of privacy practices throughout the period [date] to [date].

Description of tests of controls

The specific controls and privacy commitments tested and the nature, timing, and results of those tests are listed on pages [yy–zz].

Intended use

This report and the description of tests of controls, tests of privacy commitments, and results thereof in section X of this report are intended solely for the information and use of XYZ Service Organization; user entities of XYZ Service Organization's [type or name of] system during some or all of the period [date] to [date]; and those prospective user entities, independent auditors and practitioners providing services to such user entities, and regulators who have sufficient knowledge and understanding of the following:

- The nature of the service provided by the service organization
- How the service organization's system interacts with user entities, subservice organizations, and other parties
- Internal control and its limitations
- Complementary user-entity controls and how they interact with related controls at the service organization to meet the applicable trust services criteria
- The applicable trust services criteria
- The risks that may threaten the achievement of the applicable trust services criteria and how controls address those risks

This report is not intended to be and should not be used by anyone other than these specified parties.

[*Service auditor's signature*]

[*Date of the service auditor's report*]

[*Service auditor's city and state*]

Appendix D

Definitions

For purposes of this guide, the following terms have the meanings attributed as follows:

Applicable trust services criteria. The criteria in TSP section 100, *Trust Services Principles, Criteria, and Illustrations for Security, Availability, Processing Integrity, Confidentiality, and Privacy* (AICPA, *Technical Practice Aids*), that are applicable to the principle(s) being reported on.

Boundaries of the system. The boundaries of a system are the specific aspects of a service organization's infrastructure, software, people, procedures, and data necessary to provide its services. When the systems for multiple services share aspects, infrastructure, software, people, procedures, and data, the systems will overlap, but the boundaries of each service's system will differ. In a SOC 2 engagement that addresses the privacy principle, the system boundaries cover, at a minimum, all the system components as they relate to the personal information life cycle within well-defined processes and informal ad-hoc procedures.

Carve-out method. Method of addressing the services provided by a subservice organization whereby management's description of the service organization's system identifies the nature of the services performed by the subservice organization and excludes from the description and scope of the service auditor's engagement the subservice organization's controls to meet the applicable trust services criteria. The description of the service organization's system and the scope of the engagement include controls at the service organization that monitor the effectiveness of controls at the subservice organization, which may include the service organization's review of a servicer auditor's report on controls at the subservice organization.

Complementary user-entity controls. Controls that management assumes, in the design of the service provided by the service organization, will be implemented by user entities and that, if necessary to achieve the applicable trust services criteria, are identified as such in that description.

Controls at a service organization. The policies and procedures at a service organization that are likely to be relevant to user entities' internal control, as they relate to meeting the applicable trust services criteria. These policies and procedures are designed, implemented, and documented by the service organization to provide reasonable assurance about meeting the applicable trust services criteria.

Controls at a subservice organization. The policies and procedures at a subservice organization that are likely to be relevant to user entities of the service organization, as they relate to meeting the applicable trust services criteria. These policies and procedures are designed, implemented, and documented by the subservice organization to provide reasonable assurance about meeting the applicable trust services criteria.

Criteria. The standards or benchmarks used to measure and present the subject matter and against which the practitioner evaluates the subject matter.

Data subjects. The individuals about whom personal information is collected.

Inclusive method. Method of addressing the services provided by a subservice organization whereby the service organization's description of its system includes a description of the nature of the services provided by the subservice organization, as well as the subservice organization's controls to meet the applicable trust services criteria.

Management's assertion. A written assertion by management of a service organization or management of a subservice organization, if applicable, about the matters referred to in paragraph 1.16(a)(ii)(1)–(4) of this guide for a type 2 report and the matters referred to in paragraph 1.16(b)(ii)(1)–(2)of this guide for a type 1 report.

Personal information life cycle. The collection, use, retention, disclosure, disposal, or anonymization of personal information within well-defined processes and informal ad hoc procedures.

Privacy notice. A written communication by entities that collect personal information to the individuals about whom personal information is collected about the entity's (*a*) policies regarding the nature of the information that they will collect and how that information will be used, retained, disclosed, and disposed of or anonymized and (*b*) the entity's commitment to adhere to those policies. A privacy notice also includes information about such matters as the purpose of collecting the information, the choices that individuals have related to their personal information, the security of such information, and how individuals can contact the entity with inquiries, complaints, and disputes related to their personal information. When a user entity collects personal information from individuals, it typically provides a privacy notice to those individuals.

Service auditor. A CPA who reports on the fairness of the presentation of a service organization's description of its system; the suitability of the design of controls included in the description; and in a type 2 report, the operating effectiveness of those controls to meet the applicable trust services criteria. When the report addresses the privacy principle, the service auditor also reports on the service organization's compliance with the commitments in its statement of privacy practices.

Service organization. An organization or segment of an organization that provides services to user entities related to the applicable trust services criteria.

Statement of privacy practices. A written communication by the service organization to the user entities that includes the same types of privacy policies and commitments that are included in a privacy notice (see the definition of **privacy notice**). It is written from the perspective of the service organization and is provided to the user entities when the service organization is involved in any of the phases of the personal information life cycle, and the user entity, rather than the service organization, is responsible for providing the privacy notice. A statement of privacy practices provides a basis for the user entities to prepare a privacy notice to be sent to individuals or for ensuring that the service organization has appropriate practices for meeting the existing privacy commitments of user entities. The criteria for the content of a statement of privacy practices are set forth in TSP section 100.

Subservice provider. A service organization used by another service organization to perform services related to the applicable trust services criteria.

Tests of compliance with commitments in the statement of privacy practices. Procedures designed to help provide reasonable assurance of detecting material noncompliance with the service organization's commitments related to privacy.

Test of controls. A procedure designed to evaluate the operating effectiveness of controls in meeting the applicable trust services criteria.

User entity. An entity that uses a service organization.

Appendix E

Reporting on Controls at a Cloud Computing Service Organization

This appendix describes cloud computing service organizations and provides an overview of the risks and challenges associated with performing a service organization controls (SOC) 2 engagement for cloud service organizations.

A cloud computing service organization (cloud service organization) provides user entities with on-demand access to a shared pool of configuarable computing resources (for example, networks, servers, storage, and applications). Cloud computing is becoming an important IT strategy for user entities that need varying levels of IT resources and for whom purchasing and maintaining sophisticated and costly IT resources is not an effective strategy.

Definition of *Cloud Computing*

Although many definitions of the term *cloud computing* exist, the following definition from the National Institute of Standards and Technology (NIST)[1] is widely used:

Cloud computing is a model for enabling convenient, on-demand network access to a shared pool of configurable computing resources (e.g., networks, servers, storage, applications, and services) that can be rapidly provisioned and released with minimal management effort or service provider interaction. This cloud model promotes availability and is composed of five essential **characteristics**, three **service models**, and four **deployment models**.

Essential Characteristics:

- *On-demand self-service.* A consumer can unilaterally provision computing capabilities, such as server time and network storage, as needed automatically without requiring human interaction with each service's provider.
- *Broad network access.* Capabilities are available over the network and accessed through standard mechanisms that promote use by heterogeneous thin or thick client platforms (e.g., mobile phones, laptops, and PDAs).
- *Resource pooling.* The provider's computing resources are pooled to serve multiple consumers using a multi-tenant model, with different physical and virtual resources dynamically assigned and reassigned according to consumer

---

[1] Mell, Peter and Tim Grance, "The NIST Definition of Cloud Computing," Version 15 (October 7, 2009) http://csrc.nist.gov/groups/SNS/cloud-computing/.

demand. There is a sense of location independence in that the customer generally has no control or knowledge over the exact location of the provided resources but may be able to specify location at a higher level of abstraction (e.g., country, state, or datacenter). Examples of resources include storage, processing, memory, network bandwidth, and virtual machines.

- *Rapid elasticity.* Capabilities can be rapidly and elastically provisioned, in some cases automatically, to quickly scale out and rapidly released to quickly scale in. To the consumer, the capabilities available for provisioning often appear to be unlimited and can be purchased in any quantity at any time.

- *Measured service.* Cloud systems automatically control and optimize resource use by leveraging a metering capability at some level of abstraction appropriate to the type of service (e.g., storage, processing, bandwidth, and active user accounts). Resource usage can be monitored, controlled, and reported providing transparency for both the provider and consumer of the utilized service.

Service Models:

- *Cloud Software as a Service (SaaS).* The capability provided to the consumer is to use the provider's applications running on a cloud infrastructure. The applications are accessible from various client devices through a thin client interface such as a web browser (e.g., web-based email). The consumer does not manage or control the underlying cloud infrastructure including network, servers, operating systems, storage, or even individual application capabilities, with the possible exception of limited user-specific application configuration settings.

- *Cloud Platform as a Service (PaaS).* The capability provided to the consumer is to deploy onto the cloud infrastructure consumer-created or acquired applications created using programming languages and tools supported by the provider. The consumer does not manage or control the underlying cloud infrastructure including network, servers, operating systems, or storage, but has control over the deployed applications and possibly application hosting environment configurations.

- *Cloud Infrastructure as a Service (IaaS).* The capability provided to the consumer is to provision processing, storage, networks, and other fundamental computing resources where the consumer is able to deploy and run arbitrary software, which can include operating systems and applications. The consumer does not manage or control the underlying cloud infrastructure but has control over operating systems, storage, deployed applications, and possibly limited control of select networking components (e.g., host firewalls).

Deployment Models:

- *Private cloud.* The cloud infrastructure is operated solely for an organization. It may be managed by the organization or a third party and may exist on premise or off premise.

- *Community cloud.* The cloud infrastructure is shared by several organizations and supports a specific community that has shared concerns (e.g., mission, security requirements, policy, and compliance considerations). It may be managed by the organizations or a third party and may exist on premise or off premise.

- *Public cloud.* The cloud infrastructure is made available to the general public or a large industry group and is owned by an organization selling cloud services.

- *Hybrid cloud.* The cloud infrastructure is a composition of two or more clouds (private, community, or public) that remain unique entities but are bound together by standardized or proprietary technology that enables data and application portability (e.g., cloud bursting for load-balancing between clouds).

Risks to User Entities

Although management of a user entity may outsource the IT functions to a cloud service organization, it cannot outsource its responsibility for the operations of those functions. As a result, management of a user entity may need to actively monitor and assess aspects of the cloud service organization's system that affect the services provided to the user entity. The very characteristics that make cloud computing an attractive solution may also increase certain risks to the user entities. For example

- the increased sharing of system resources among user entities increases the risk that the activities of one user entity will adversely affect the availability, security, processing integrity, confidentiality, and privacy of the other user entities.

- the essential characteristics of cloud computing make it difficult to assess whether the cloud service organization is fulfilling certain commitments related to confidentiality and privacy that it has made to user entities, such as in contracts, service level agreements, or statements of privacy practices. For example, a cloud service organization may reallocate online data storage space between user entities to address the changing demands for resources. In these circumstances, the second user entity may be able to access the data of the original user of the storage space, unless the cloud service organization has controls to erase that data from the storage space.

- the aggregation of many user entities' data in a single cloud environment increases the attractiveness of the cloud computing organization as a target for attacks, given the extent of data that can potentially be compromised and misused.

- cloud providers spawn and retire virtual servers regularly to respond to changing user-entity demands. The transitory nature of these virtual servers increases the risk that unauthorized system changes are introduced in the respawning processes (bringing the server up again). In addition, this transitory nature increases the risk that traditional audit trails (for example, system logs or configuration reports) will not provide sufficient evidence of the functioning of controls for the cloud-based systems.

- the dynamic nature of cloud computing can result in the data being stored on different physical storage devices using different data security controls. As a result, data security controls designed with the assumption that data is stored in a static location may not be effective.

Challenges Faced by the Cloud Service Organization in Meeting Users' Information Needs

In order for management of a user entity to actively monitor and assess aspects of the cloud service organization's system that affect the services provided to the user entity, it will need information about the service organization's system. In providing such information, the cloud service organization faces many of the traditional challenges faced by service organizations, including the following:

- Controlling the cost and disruption resulting from inquiries and visits from multiple user entities who wish to obtain information about the system and test system controls that are relevant to those user entities. Adding to such costs and disruption is the time required to train user entity personnel about cloud services, processes, and architecture.

- Balancing the need to protect user entities' information against the need to provide governance, risk, and control information to existing and prospective user entities. For example, providing a user entity with detailed security configuration information regarding the cloud environment increases the risk that personnel at that user entity will use that information to compromise security and gain access to other user entities' data.

- Balancing the need to provide information about the system to user entities in an effective and efficient manner against the need to protect the cloud service organization from risks, such as the disclosure of confidential user-entity information. For example, in a traditional data center setting, a user entity usually has access to all data and system resources for a dedicated e-mail server. If a cloud computing architecture comingles e-mails from multiple users in a single database, providing such access to all data and system resources in a cloud setting would compromise the confidentiality of other user entities' e-mail.

A service auditor's SOC 2 report can be an effective tool for communicating information about the cloud service organization's services and the suitability of the design and operating effectiveness of controls over the systems that provides these services. It can provide assurance to existing and prospective user entities regarding the service organization's services, including confidence in the security, availability, and processing integrity of the system and controls over data confidentiality and privacy of information. This additional confidence can help the cloud service organization address the concerns of prospective and existing customers in a consistent and comprehensive manner, rather than having to customize a response to specific requirements of different user entities. In a new and developing industry, such confidence can help increase the rate of adoption of a cloud service organization's services and the extent to which user entities are willing to trust critical operations to the cloud environment.

Risk Considerations When Performing a SOC 2 Engagement for a Cloud Service Organization

Performing a SOC 2 engagement for a cloud service organization is conceptually the same as performing such an engagement for any other service organization that provides IT services. However, when performing these engagements, the service auditor needs to pay particular attention to matters such as the following:

- *Shared responsibility.* The responsibility for controls is shared between the user entities and service organization. One challenge of providing cloud services is that different user entities will often require varying levels of service and related responsibility and accountability on the part of the cloud service organization. In these situations, the service auditor needs to consider the processes and controls that the cloud service organization has in place to address the differing requirements of its user entities.

- *Information life cycle management when reporting on confidentiality and privacy.* Information life cycle management is one of the most challenging aspects of managing a cloud, particularly when addressing privacy requirements. Because cloud service organizations have multiple clients sharing system resources, and these shared resources (for example, servers and storage devices) may be reallocated among the clients depending on needs at a given time, information life cycle management for any particular client may become highly complex and challenging to administer.

- *Comingling of data when reporting on confidentiality and privacy.* Many SaaS environments comingle the data of user entities in a single database. As a result, it may be difficult to completely destroy or return user entity data at the end of its life cycle or at the end of the relationship between a user entity and cloud service provider.

- *Transnational data processing and storage.* Many types of data, including personal information, are subject to specific laws and regulations in the jurisdiction in which the data is created or in which the data subject is a resident of, including restrictions on the transfer of data to other jurisdictions. Cloud service providers may be unaware of the particular requirements for any one user entity, and the multinational architecture of a cloud infrastructure may result in unintended violations of laws and regulations by the user entity.

- *Availability, continuity of operations, and disaster recovery when reporting on availability.* Cloud computing environments are inherently complex due to the need to support multiple clients with varying system requirements (for example, different operating systems and virtual servers) and variations in the demand for resources among clients. Due to this complexity, techniques for maintaining system availability, providing for continuity of operations when a disruption has occurred, and recovering from a disaster vary significantly from traditional techniques. The flexibility provided by cloud architecture usually provides the cloud with the technological ability to recover user entity processing on different hardware operating in the same or a different facility but requires more complex processes and controls to do so.

- *Virtualization technologies.* Although not unique to a cloud, the implementation, configuration, protection, operation, and support of virtualization hypervisors is critical to most cloud computing environments. A *hypervisor* is a software program that manages multiple operating systems on a single computer system. Hypervisors need to be configured and managed to meet the combined security, availability, and processing integrity needs of customers. A service auditor needs to understand the hypervisor(s) used by the cloud service organization and the unique policies, procedures, and processes used to configure and maintain them. The service auditor also needs to address the same issues with regard to any applications or software infrastructure provided in a multitenancy environment.

- *Transitory nature of virtual environments.* Because of the virtual nature of individual user-entity processing environments and the highly dynamic nature of resource allocation, traditional testing strategies related to system configuration may not provide sufficient evidence about the operating effectiveness of controls. Similarly, audit evidence traditionally used to evaluate the operation of the control may not exist or may not be sufficiently reliable when testing in a cloud environment. The service auditor needs to give consideration to these factors in planning and performing his or her examination.

- *Encryption and key management.*[2] Encryption is generally an effective way of protecting information in a cloud computing environment. Encryption of data may be the responsibility of the user entity, cloud service organization, or both and may vary from user entity to user entity within any one cloud computing environment. A cloud service organization needs to have processes and controls in place to meet its responsibilities, in accordance with service level agreements. In addition, processes and controls are needed to protect encryption keys during key generation, storage, use, change, and destruction.

---

[2] *Encryption* is a form of security that turns information, images, programs, or other data into unreadable cipher by applying a set of complex algorithms to the original material. These algorithms transfer the data into streams or blocks of seemingly random alphanumeric characters. An encryption key might encrypt, decrypt, or perform both functions, depending on the type of encryption software being used.

Engagement Acceptance Considerations for the Service Auditor

Prior to accepting an engagement to report on controls at a service organization related to the trust services principles, a practitioner should consider whether he or she has the necessary skills and knowledge to perform the examination or will need to use the work of a specialist with the necessary skills and knowledge.

In performing a SOC 2 engagement for a cloud service organization, a service auditor needs to consider the following:

- Whether the cloud environment is private, public, community, or hybrid and the different risks that each deployment model brings to the environment.

- Whether the description is sufficient to meet the needs of user entities based on industry and regulatory considerations. The cloud service provider's description of its system should address unique aspects that cloud computing brings to common processes, including the following:

  — Data governance

  — Information leakage

  — Hardware disposal

  — Hypervisor security and change control

  — Spawning and retirement of virtual systems

  — Encryption

  — Incident management

  — Use of third parties

  Because of the rapidly evolving nature of cloud computing, service auditors should consider consulting the publications and online resources of organizations that address cloud computing, including the NIST, the European Network and Information Security Agency, and the Cloud Security Alliance (CSA).

- When reporting on privacy in a cloud environment, how privacy risks are affected by the shared aspects of a cloud environment, including the following:

  — Privacy policies and notices

  — Breach notice

  — Access

  — Regulatory requirements

  — The types of personal information in the cloud environment and its sensitivity

  — Sharing of information with third parties

- Whether the controls identified are sufficiently responsive to the applicable trust services criteria, given the dynamic nature of cloud computing and the particular risks associated with it.

- Whether the results of tests of controls will be sufficient to support the auditor's opinion, given the dynamic nature of infrastructure considerations. For example, security configurations of hypervisors and servers are subject to frequent modification throughout the period. Tests that infer the operating effectiveness of controls through inspection of the results of their operation (for example, inspection of security configuration files) are likely to be less effective, unless performed throughout the report period using a statistical-based sampling approach.

Cloud Security Frameworks

Due to the immaturity and rapid growth of cloud computing, cloud service organizations and their user entities are still refining the security processes and controls that should be in place at the service organization. To aid in this effort, cloud service organizations and user entities have joined together with governmental bodies in several different efforts to develop frameworks for assessing risks, processes, and controls for a cloud environment. Implementation of a framework could be demonstrated by a SOC 2 report in which the description of the system includes descriptions of the framework used, the processes designed to address the framework requirements, and controls implemented in response to the framework requirements.

One leading framework has been developed by the CSA. This framework consists of the following:

- Consensus assessment questions that have been developed to help user entities gather information relevant to the security and availability of a cloud service provider's system
- Common controls matrix that provides cloud service providers and user entities with illustrative controls

More information on the CSA framework can be found at https://cloudsecurityalliance.org/.

———————————